We h ... of this
br ... Like
...)lves
... ;s.

... 'e

Here the reader may consider new theories, new plans, and practices; he may evaluate the tasks that face educators and administrators; and, most important, he may—perhaps for the first time—come to grips with the formidable barriers that block change in today's schools—and in tomorrow's.

ABOUT THE AUTHOR

DONALD F. CAY earned his M.Ed. and Ed.D from the University of Florida, where he held a fellowship in Secondary Education. He has taught at the University of Florida and at the Women's College of Georgia, and is currently Associate Professor of Education at Western Illinois University.

CURRICULUM:
design for learning

DONALD F. CAY

Western Illinois University

The BOBBS-MERRILL Company, Inc.
A subsidiary of Howard W. Sams & Co., Inc.
Publishers · Indianapolis · New York · Kansas City

To My Wife,
VIRGINIA

PREFACE

This book on curriculum is different from the standard treatment of the subject. Although it clearly recognizes the importance of subject matter, the emphasis is on people and their influences upon the curriculum. The emphasis is upon what happens in curriculum building—on people, on processes, and on the mechanics of change. It is assumed that curriculum changes as people change, and this book attempts to delineate ways in which people may affect the curriculum as they change their practices, beliefs, goals, and values.

Many professional educators and academic specialists have contributed to the understanding of curriculum by giving detailed explanations of the academic areas that make up the instructional portion of curriculum. It is with due respect and acknowledgement to these persons that the author places the major emphasis in curriculum building in a different sphere, and gives a general overview of curriculum-building processes, not an encyclopedic treatment of the subject. By design, this is an introductory work in curriculum improvement and should be used in such a framework. Those professional persons who aim toward curriculum leadership positions should deepen their understandings beyond the level of this text.

One of the most fascinating aspects of the growth and development of public schools in America is the curriculum. As America has gone through successive evolutionary stages, from frontier country to urban settlements, the public-school curriculum has reflected the shifting values and emphases that have been a part of this process. American educators, from kindergarten through the university level, have always been dedicated to the task of producing the best possible future citizens for our nation. It is no less credit to them that they have not always reached their goal.

Attempting to build better curriculums is no easy job. There are no panaceas, no short cuts, no easy roads to better curriculums. The task requires knowledge, skill, fortitude, and faith in youth and their educability today for a brighter and better world of tomorrow. Such faith is the stock in trade of most educators, for they teach with their eyes on the future. Building better curriculums and working closely with young people is a future-oriented professional responsibility. The educator's contribution today may not have its fruition until twenty years from now. Although the educator may never be aware of his specific influence on his pupil, he is aware of his potential contribution. As a major professional responsibility, he seeks to improve the curriculum so that the generation of students he teaches may find greater fulfillment than any preceding one.

The field of curriculum and instruction has become a highly specialized area of study and endeavor. In order that this field may offer the leadership necessary to growth and improvement in public education, many changes in methods of current school operation are essential. These basic changes will involve long-term approaches to our school problems, careful and forward-looking planning, intelligent use of research findings, wise utilization of staff creativity, intelligent use of physical facilities, experimental programs, and continuous evaluation of all educational experiences.

As academic subject matter grows and changes within specific disciplines, so must the methods of presentation and the use of instructional aids grow and change. Acceptance of change simply for the sake of change cannot be tolerated. New ways of teaching and learning must show promise of better results. If we want evidence of improved performance before adoption of new techniques, then we must create more experimental learning situations. Public schools, at all levels, will need to promote experimentation with the support and encouragement of their communities.

In attempting to develop some guidelines for curriculum building that can be understood and practiced by educators and interested laymen, this book offers an analysis of the human aspects and processes of curriculum. The book tries to show some of the roles played by persons, institutions, and social forces in shaping curriculum design. It also points out some basic requirements of better curriculums as well as some of the difficulties encountered and barriers involved in curriculum building. Its use is intended to stimulate the reader to thought and action that will be directed toward improved curriculums. After achieving a beginning, basic understanding of the human processes and barriers involved in curriculum building, it is hoped that the reader will want to assist in the creation of a better curriculum.

March 1965   D. F. C.

CONTENTS

CURRICULUM:
design for learning

I

WHAT IS CURRICULUM?

Curriculum is the educational design of learning experiences for children, youth, and adults in school. It is people and their value systems, their beliefs, their philosophies, and their practices regarding education. It is educators and parents working together for the improvement of the educational program. It is the reflection of political, religious, social, and ethical values of any given society in its school systems. The living curriculum is school experience involving interaction between those who teach and those who learn.

"Curriculum" is the professional educational term that covers school experiences like an umbrella. Name any facet of school activity you like, and it will be included in a modern concept of the term *curriculum*. It is the master plan, devised by educators and other adults in a community, state, or nation that will best serve their needs, and, as they see it, the needs of their children. It consists of a preconceived design of educational experiences that should lead to desired goals, eventually benefiting the individual and the society.

As in all enterprises, educational or otherwise, a moving force or personality is necessary to put the design into action. In curriculum, the moving force is the classroom teacher. It is in the context of teacher-pupil interaction, on a daily basis, that life is breathed into the preconceived design we call curriculum.

Curriculum is an individual matter with individual pupils. Although a classroom teacher may present the same material to all pupils, each individual interprets the material in the light of his own experience, which is unique. Actually a teacher gives direction and motivation to many different curriculums each day. In the final analysis, curriculum is people and the ways in which they interact with each other in a school situation.

One cannot minimize what is taught nor why it is taught. Neither can one place undue emphasis upon how it is taught, yet it is in the context of "how" that an individual pupil's curriculum comes to life for him. On the basis of research and experience in teaching, most teachers would agree that one cannot divorce subject matter from the personality of the teacher. In the specialized area of curriculum, one cannot separate the content or method from the personalities of those who teach.

Courses of study, study guides, suggested units of work, workshops and conferences all help the classroom teacher gain a sense of direction. Professional organizations, in their meetings, offer new ideas to teachers. Writers in the field of education suggest new ways of approaching the various learning tasks. As helpful as all of these resources may be to the classroom teachers, the curriculum comes to life as teachers and pupils interact in the school. The individual classroom is the testing ground. Here is where all of the ideas, knowledge, techniques, and understandings of the teacher crystallize into action, and the living curriculum is born. Prior to this time, the curriculum is a printed document formed by the minds and experiences of educators and lay citizens.

Where does the professional term *curriculum* come from? As is often the case, when one looks at the etymology of a word, some humor is involved. The term *curriculum* had its origin in Latin, spelled "curriculum" in its singular form and "curricula" in its plural. Its adjectival form is "curricular." Current usage permits an Anglicized plural form of "curriculums," and this is the plural form that is used throughout this book.

The original Latin meaning of curriculum was "a running course or race course, especially a chariot race course." From Latin, the word passed into French as the verb *courir*, meaning "to run." Combining the Latin and French meanings, one deduces that curriculum could mean "to run a race course," with or without the chariot, although the dictionary definition is "a course; especially a fixed course of study, as in a school or college, as one leading to a degree."[1]

If one examined closely the courses of study offered by many of our public schools and colleges, he might feel justified in concluding that pupils are indeed running a race, without the benefit of chariot, from entrance into elementary school through completion of graduate degrees at the university level. The strongest emphasis in American education from 1860–1964 has been on the "fixed" or "prescribed" course of study. This emphasis is the major factor that has caused many educators to condemn the "lock step" pattern of courses our youth must follow at the secondary level. In looking squarely at our fixed courses of study, one is forced to admit that the amount of creativity a pupil encounters in the classroom is likely to be accidental or coincidental, rather than an integral part of planned learning experiences. To encourage potential creativity as a vital part of daily learning for youth is a major task of curriculum builders.

It is exceedingly difficult to find any other definition of curriculum that will be accepted by everybody. There are, however, four definitions that have gained wide acceptance among educators:

a. The curriculum is made up of subject-matter courses, arranged in logical sequences.
b. The curriculum consists of planned learning experiences to bring about changed behavior patterns in pupils.
c. Curriculum is the design of a social group for the educational experiences of their children in school.[2]
d. Curriculum consists of all the experiences of the learners— what they undergo, feel, and react to under the guidance of the school.[3]

These four definitions and the original definition by the author show an awareness of the physical, mental, and emotional nature of

[1]*Webster's Unabridged Dictionary*, 2nd. ed. (Springfield, Mass.: G. & C. Merriam Co., 1959).

[2]George A. Beauchamp, *Planning the Elementary School Curriculum* (Boston: Allyn-Bacon, Inc., 1956), p. 1.

[3]*The Work of the Curriculum Coordinator in Selected New Jersey Schools* (New York: Bureau of Publications, Teachers College, Columbia University, 1955), p. 2.

pupils. They also illustrate the sociological nature of the school as an institution, in addition to its function as the source of planned academic learning experiences. Think for a moment of the daily routine of a pupil in school. He does many things simply out of necessity. Most of the contrived learning experiences of school, for example, have to be undergone by the pupil for the teacher's benefit. These experiences, for the most part, are of the adult's making—not the child's. The pupil also has many different feelings each day regarding himself, his teachers, and his classmates. These feelings may range all the way from exultation to withdrawal, depending on the pupil's perception of the situation. Whether the method in which a pupil reacts to daily school experience is openly expressed, or suppressed for the sake of avoiding difficulty with the teacher, one may be sure that he is reacting to his environment and experiences of the classroom.

Listening to a group of pupils as they move down a hall from one part of a school building to another or from the building to a play area removes any doubt of the fact that they do react. They react to teachers, learning experiences, classmates, and other school groups. These pupils, who are the *raison d'être* for the curriculum, possess a large amount of active energy which they expend—one way or another—each day. One of the major tasks of schools and teachers is to attempt to build curriculums that will enable the pupils to channel their energies into constructive living and learning experiences whenever possible.

In the light of recent findings concerning how people learn—for example, the effects upon learning of emotions and sociological factors—there is much room for improvement in most schools and the curriculums they build. A keen observer of contemporary schools, attempting to evaluate the school's use of available modern knowledge in its curriculum, says, "All our schools are obsolescent."[4] This observation was not made to condemn our schools, but rather to make them acutely aware of the tremendous potential for improvement that lies in the application of available modern knowl-

[4]Herbert A. Thelen, *Education and the Human Quest* (New York: Harper & Brothers, 1960), p. 1.

edge. Perhaps we have been placing too much emphasis on skill building, and not nearly enough on assisting pupils to find personal meaning in their search for self and to build satisfying relationships with others. As necessary as skills are as working tools in the search for self, they may well become a secondary factor in the curriculums of tomorrow. To help pupils find real meaning, in a personal sense, from the knowledge they gain in school may well be the most legitimate goal for future curriculums.

If we are to help pupils find meaning for themselves from knowledge and experience gained in school, then we must encourage them to test and experiment with their new-found knowledge on a daily basis. Much of the learning going on in classrooms today is of an intellectual, hypothetical nature as the pupils see it, whereas they are more inclined to assimilate learning that contains active participation by them. Emphasis should be given by educators to more actual doing in the classroom—the kind of doing that actively involves learners in the accomplishment of specific tasks.

There is considerable comment today about the need for a revolution in public education. One can scarcely disagree with the intent of this statement, insofar as it indicates a recognition of the need for educational change. However, educational change is a part of social change, which has often been aptly described as extremely slow. Social change is an integral part of our culture and moves at the pace of an inchworm. If one is to judge future progress in social change by what has happened in the past, educators will have to be satisfied with evolutionary changes in educational practice—not revolutionary ones. There is no need to discourage a revolutionary new approach to our educational problems, on the theoretical level, for the time is right for such a move. One should point out, however, that even though revolutionary thinking is applied to educational problems, the implementation of theory into practice in the schools will be of an evolutionary nature. If educators can learn to be satisfied with gradual change in classroom practices and to assist the public to change its conception of the role and function of the school, better curriculums can and will be built in future cooperative ventures.

In the past, the schools, parents, and other lay citizens of the community have not worked together as closely as possible. Schools have often been justly accused of being "little islands" or "ivory towers." Schools have frequently invited citizens to visit only when there is a special program, such as a band concert, art exhibit, or dramatic production. The things adults have missed have been those that take place in the classroom and help to show new ways of working with pupils and new content. One of the most pressing needs as we strive to design and build better curriculums is for educators and lay citizens of communities to learn to work together successfully. The late Henry Ford, in reference to human relations, stated this need very succinctly:

> Coming together is a beginning,
> Keeping together is progress,
> Working together is success.[5]

Where do adults get their ideas about the schools? The only real conception of the schools that many adults have is a memory of the schools of twenty to forty years ago when they were pupils. Their own personal experience with school may have been happy or unhappy. Their evaluations of public schools and the curriculums today, praiseworthy or critical, are often based on memory, dimmed and altered by the years. One of the prime objectives of educators is to help adults change and modernize their conceptions of the school, its curriculum, and its methods of implementing the curriculum. Accomplishment of this objective will require close working relationships between educators and adult citizens of the communities served by the school.

Curriculum design represents a complex of interrelated factors: persons, places, and things. Building a curriculum is much like putting together the pieces of a jig-saw puzzle. Even when the many parts of a curriculum are put together to form a design, the curriculum, unlike the jig-saw puzzle, must be subject to continual scrutiny, re-evaluation, and change by its architects.

Fields of knowledge are expanding and changing rapidly today,

[5]Henry Ford quoted in Gerald L. Timm, "Public Relations and Business Education," *The Balance Sheet* (December 1959), p. 161.

more rapidly than they ever have in the past. The curriculum that served for a generation of Americans in the 1920's or the 1940's can hardly be expected to serve for the new generations of the 1960's or 1980's. One of the greatest weaknesses of curriculums of the past has been their static nature. Change itself needs to be accepted as a welcome ally and constant companion by those who build curriculums. There are few things of which we may be sure with respect to the future, but the phenomenon of change is one thing we can count on. We are just beginning, for instance, to scratch the surface of a whole new world of travel and exploration in space. The curriculums of the future cannot be static if they are to serve adequately the youth who enters a world where rocketry, telemetry, and atomic energy will become as commonplace as the biplane, telegraphy, and electric power of the early years of this century. The design of curriculums of the future will have to be flexible enough to admit entirely new areas of knowledge as they appear. Although the curriculum of colonial America was designed for the man on horseback, the curriculum of today and tomorrow must be designed for potential astronauts.

SOURCES OF CURRICULUM

So far we have tried to gain an understanding of what the curriculum is and different ways of defining it. We have also looked at some suggestions concerning possible future development of curriculums. Before we go further in our study of how people build better curriculums, we need to examine the potential sources of curriculum. We should more genuinely appreciate the task before us if we know where one must look for ideas, academic content, values, methods, and techniques needed to improve present curriculums. What are the potential basic sources of curriculum?

Herrick has stated that the following three areas are the basic sources:

There are only three basic referents or orientations possible to consider in the development of distinctive curriculum patterns and in the making of many pivotal curriculum decisions. These three referents are: man's categorized and preserved knowledge—subject fields; our society, its institutions and social processes; and the individual to be educated—his nature, needs, and developmental patterns.[6]

Many other authorities in the field of curriculum would add additional categories or devise slightly different labels; however, most of them would agree that curriculums must be based on all three of these orientations. In looking for sources for curriculum building, we can turn to the subject fields, the society, and the individual.

Advances, revisions, innovations, and changes in public-school curriculums have alternately proceeded on one of these three lines of approach. Most recently we have been quite deeply involved in curriculum revisions stemming from the subject-fields approach. National committees of academic specialists and professional educators have worked closely with secondary-school teachers to revise and reform high-school courses in certain academic areas. Most notable among the curriculums reformed have been those in the fields of mathematics, science, and foreign languages. Additional national studies have been undertaken in English, social sciences, and humanities. Further curriculum reforms will be forthcoming in these and other fields of study.

Curriculum builders of the past have relied, for the most part, on one or the other of these three areas of concentration as they attempted to improve curriculums. In the colonial schools the emphasis was upon the subject fields and religion. Social needs were paramount in the planning of curriculums for some schools in the early years of this century. More recently, great emphasis has been directed to the individual and his needs as the basic core of curriculum planning. Most recently has come the renewed emphasis upon reforming the subject-matter content of the public-school curriculum.

We have come a very long distance since those early days in the history of American schools. Schools and their curriculums are better today than they have ever been. A great part of the pressure

[6]Virgil E. Herrick, "Sources of Curriculum Development," *What Are the Sources of the Curriculum? A Symposium* (Washington: Association for Supervision and Curriculum Development, 1962), p. 61.

to reform curriculums from the subject-field approach has been brought on by the tremendous increase in knowledge itself. As Goodlad illustrates this phenomenon, we can see that contemporary curriculum builders must work on subject fields:

... it is estimated that the first doubling of knowledge occurred in 1750, the second in 1900, the third in 1950, and the fourth in 1960. Whether or not these are only rough approximations, they have impressed upon educators an inescapable fact, well stated by Professor Schwab of the University of Chicago: "It is no longer merely difficult to select and package for instruction the most important bits and pieces of knowledge; it is impossible! The search is on for something more lasting than 'the bits and pieces' emerging as a residue from the advance of knowledge, something more permanent around which to organize learning."[7]

With the available sum of knowledge in the world doubling itself in the ten-year period between 1950 and 1960, the pressure was on for increased academic competency and updating of content to try to keep the schools on a par with the explosion of knowledge. The two major explosions we have had to try to deal with in this generation have been those of population and knowledge. One affects the other, and both have a profound influence upon the schools. An appropriate example of the combined effects of the population and knowledge increases may be offered by looking at recent methods of grouping pupils. Large-group instruction is very popular today, and increasingly more mechanical and audio-visual aids are used to try to reach these large groups. Instructional television is used on a closed circuit basis in some public schools to try to bring an excellently qualified teacher to a very large group of pupils. All types of projectors are common for use with large groups. Teaching machines code and program some bits and segments of knowledge to assist pupils to learn on their own and thus free teachers for other instructional tasks. Machines, in the form of electronic computers, codify and recall some items of the huge masses of available information. Every known effort is being made to keep up with the knowledge

[7]John I. Goodlad, "The Changing Curriculum of America's Schools," *Saturday Review* (November 16, 1963), p. 65.

and population explosions. Some teachers are being helped by machines, team teaching, instructional aids, and clerical assistants in their battle to devote more of their professional time and talent to teaching their specialized area. A major attempt is being made to reduce the amount of time teachers must devote to clerical tasks and to free them for creative teaching.

SUBJECT FIELDS AS A SOURCE OF CURRICULUM

The sense of urgency regarding new knowledge plunges the educator into a very real dilemma when it comes to selecting content from the subject fields. The rapid increase in knowledge in many fields in the last ten years has compounded the problem of selection of specific content. There has always been more knowledge available than any pupil could learn in the time allotted to school work. Today, however, the accumulation of knowledge has become so overwhelming that one is forced to develop a series of priorities in knowledge. For a time, as a result of Russia's successfully orbiting the first satellite, a clear-cut priority was given in this country to mathematics, science, and foreign languages. Today, however, calls are being made for more widespread inclusion of other subjects to keep the curriculum balanced.

Educators and parents need to work together and make some decisions regarding what seems to be most important for youth to learn during their public-school years. The basic skills of reading, writing, and arithmetic are just as important today as ever before; in fact, perhaps even more important than ever before. New knowledge means that something has to give somewhere in the curriculum. Some old concepts and techniques will need to be sloughed off to make room for the new.

The expert academician, in any one of the subject fields, can offer considerable assistance to parents and professional educators as they attempt to develop priorities for content. The college subject-field specialists have given leadership to the national curriculum studies of the past ten years and can be counted on in the future to help curriculum-planning groups.

Teachers, administrators, professional educators, and academic specialists can begin to build better curriculums by making the necessary priority decisions in subject-fields areas. What is to be included and how much on each specific level of learning—the scope and sequence of the instructional program—is one decision that must be made as a foundation for all other curriculum dimensions.

THE SOCIETY AS A SOURCE OF CURRICULUM

In attempting to find sources upon which to draw for the content and experiences of the curriculum, the needs of the society in which the school exists cannot be ignored. The school is basically, from the historical point of view, an agency of the society for the transmission of its cultural heritage and values. Each society, in its own time and in its own way, has had problems that loomed as major obstacles to progress. Today's society in America, no less than other societies in other places and other times, has many problems that the school can help to solve. Notice that we said the school can *help* to solve these social problems. We do not believe that the school can or should solve them alone. Future progress in the solution of social problems will be assisted by a joint, cooperative attack by all the community agencies dedicated to their resolution. The school is *one agency*, not the only one.

A major problem—and a complicated one—that faces educators today is deciding which parts of our cultural heritage should be transmitted. Ours is a rapidly changing society and gives every indication of continuing to be so. Should we pass on all the cultural traits of the past? Are any of the old ones no longer important in today's society? Which of our cultural societal values are most necessary for future growth and stability in our country? In our search for curriculum sources, the society and its needs—present and anticipated future needs—must be taken into consideration.

If we look candidly at American society today, we may easily spot many needs. Even a casual reading of a daily newspaper makes one realize that all does not go smoothly on the American social scene. Newspapers yield stories of prejudices against ethnic groups, of unequal educational opportunities for many children, of riots and other acts of violence by teen-age groups, of school drop-outs.

What kinds of school experiences and content courses can help to solve some of these persistent problems? How can the school offer leadership to the society in attempting to assist in the resolution of problems stemming from social unrest and upheaval, poverty and disease? After all, the school does have to follow, to some extent, the pattern set for it by the society it serves; yet, it also has the responsibility to give leadership toward a better tomorrow. Will more attention to the program of citizenship development in the public schools help to erase prejudice? Or are there deeper types of interactive experiences that young people need to participate in so that they may change attitudes toward ethnic groups other than their own? Is the problem of prejudice limited to the national scene, or is it of worldwide significance today? What kinds of social values should we select to become a part of the curriculum?

We need to consider questions that have no definite answers. As we look at the successes and failures of the present society, we shall have to decide what the trend of the future seems to be. When we make this decision, we should be able to decide how we can best use school experience to inculcate and encourage the kind of thinking, feeling, and behavior that will help youth grow up to do a better job of leadership than have today's leaders. We shall have to create the kinds of social experiences in school that encourage a lessening of prejudice, a deep concern for the less fortunate, an abiding commitment to law and order, and a profound respect for democracy. There should be some school experiences where the pupil learns to place the welfare of others ahead of his own, and where he learns to sacrifice immediate personal satisfaction for later growth and development. Portions of the curriculum will have to be devoted primarily to social progress within the American and world society.

THE INDIVIDUAL AS A SOURCE OF CURRICULUM

One vital portion of our thinking and philosophy regarding public education is concerned with the fullest possible development of individual potential. We believe that each individual, within the limits of his inherited and acquired potential, should have the chance to develop himself to the highest possible level. Our schools believe this, as do our teachers, and together they implement this belief in their daily interactions with pupils. It seems quite logical that we should carefully look at what we know about the individual as one major source of curriculum.

Important factors that condition how children grow and learn have been discovered and must be taken into consideration as we try to build better curriculums. For example, children who tend to see themselves as worthy, wanted, and desirable will normally learn better than those who see themselves as unworthy, unwanted, and undesirable. Growth characteristics also have a part to play in selection of appropriate curricular experiences. Arthur Combs indicates one necessary part of the curriculum when he points out that the persons with negative self-concepts, who feel unwanted, unworthy, unable, and unacceptable, are the ones who fill jails and mental hospitals. If this is true, then helping children build positive self-concepts is a social responsibility and an essential part of the curriculum.[8]

Perhaps a major portion of our curriculums for young people who do not have positive self-concepts needs to be concerned with ways in which they may be helped to change their concepts. Many schools and communities are seriously concerned today with those pupils who have been called "disadvantaged youth" and are often dropouts. These are often the ones who most desperately need help in improving their self-concepts. Teachers and administrators will need to be patient and have understanding and empathy for these youngsters if they are to help them change their view of themselves. One writer indicates that such an emphasis in curriculum will mean individualizing instruction, re-examining grouping systems, providing challenging intellectual activity, freeing the learner to learn, helping him to trust himself and others, and freeing him to experiment with new ideas and solutions while allowing freedom to make mistakes.[9]

A curriculum based on principles such as those given above is one

[8]Arthur W. Combs, "What Can Man Become?" *California Journal for Instructional Improvement*, 4 (December 1961), 15–23.

[9]Lavone Hanna, "Meeting the Challenge," *What Are the Sources of the Curriculum?* (Washington: A.S.C.D., 1962), p. 56.

kind of curriculum that the school of the future will offer. In addition to understanding on the part of the teaching staff, considerable course work and practical experience in psychology will be required. Teachers who work in such a curriculum pattern should be trained as special-education teachers. It would seem that no other one area of concentration in curriculum building could yield greater possible returns to the individual pupil and the society than this one. On all sides today one hears and reads complaints about young people who fail to honor the laws, who seem to have little respect for themselves or others, and who appear to be headed straight toward prison or a mental institution. Teachers, well versed in dealing with youngsters who are designated as possessors of negative self-images and potential liabilities for society and themselves, may have a tremendous influence for good in re-educating these young people. With the necessary re-education, given under a very flexible curriculum with heavy emphasis upon the psychological and practical needs of these youth, the school may help to reclaim a vast amount of energy and talent.

If we can build a curriculum to aid young people to develop more positive concepts of themselves and their roles in society, then we will have accomplished a major breakthrough in public education. We can then show the public that a curriculum specifically designed to serve a special group will produce desired results. All curriculums need direction and purpose, for as Heilman indicates:

Children can grow without a professionally planned curriculum. However, the school's function is to provide guidance and direction, to structure learning situations so that certain experiences are likely to result.[10]

Up to this point we have emphasized one segment of the school population. There are other important groups of pupils who need to be served by our curriculums. There are other individual needs that should be drawn upon as curriculum sources. Some of the universal

[10]Arthur W. Heilman, *Principles and Practices of Teaching Reading* (Columbus, Ohio: Charles E. Merrill Books, Inc., 1961), p. 33.

emotional needs that the school can attempt to meet may be illustrated by the following examples:

a. The need for belonging
b. The need for achievement
c. The need for economic security
d. The need to be free from fear
e. The need for love and affection
f. The need to be free from guilt
g. The need for self-respect
h. The need for guiding purposes[11]

All of these emotional needs should be considered when one plans curriculum. Some of them may be cared for in the group environment while others may need individual attention.

We also know that individuals learn at different rates and in different ways. Some pupils learn best through seeing and doing; others through an abstract approach to new material. Our curriculums will have to be tailored so that allowances are made for the same kinds of new information to be presented in different fashions. Learning is a highly complex process and consists of many different kinds. From the social psychologists and the Freudian-oriented psychologists, we find concepts that help to explain certain behavior and learning patterns of pupils. Our understanding of the individual and his patterns of development, learning, motivation, and growth has been immeasurably increased in the past hundred years. Perhaps the next century will bring a consistent theory of human behavior and learning that will serve as a valid base for curriculum design. At present, we must choose from several different theories the best they have to offer for our specific purpose.

No one area is a sufficient base for curriculum planning today. A combination of the three basic areas—organized knowledge, society, and the individual—seems to offer the best hope for curriculum improvement. All schools cannot and should not try to produce the

[11]Louis E. Raths and Anna P. Burrell, *Do's and Don'ts of the Needs Theory*, Needs Theory Booklet, No. 2 (Bronxville, New York: Modern Education Service, 1950), pp. 3–20.

same curriculum. Some schools are so located geographically, socially, and economically that the source area they stress in curriculum building will be different from their neighbor school. Some elements of curriculum building are common to all schools; however, the curriculum source area that receives priority must be in keeping with a specific school in a specific location. This is primarily the pattern American schools have followed for a considerable period of time and thus offers one explanation for the great diversity of educational backgrounds that our high-school seniors possess.

CONTEMPORARY FORCES
AFFECTING CURRICULUM BUILDING

In designing a curriculum for the space age, the curriculum builder must be aware of the powerful contemporary forces now affecting the schools. Among these are influences as diverse as space travel, federal and state legislation, increased birth rate, desegregation, and international relations. New courses of study have been offered in mathematics, science, foreign language, vocational guidance, and human relations. Social-studies courses dealing with the problems of modern living, effective living, home and family living, and consumer education are common at the secondary-school level. As a by-product of scientific advances, automation, in the form of computers and other electronic data processing machines, audio tape recorders, video tapes, teaching machines, closed circuit television and airborne television will become increasingly important as major tools used to eradicate cultural isolation suffered by many pupils of the numerous rural schools existing in America. As the production of automated devices and machines increase, the opportunity will become available for these small rural schools to offer the same rich curriculum afforded pupils in the larger schools located in urban areas.

For more than fifty years, most rural schools have been at a distinct disadvantage because of their small size and limited finances. They could not offer the range of instructional subjects in their curriculum, as was offered by their city sisters, for the rural school could not afford to hire more staff members for such a small enrollment. Automation and television may well be a real boon to such schools in the next fifty years.

In contemporary school construction, many signs are noticeable that indicate planning of buildings and equipment designed to humanize the school environment and remove some of the institutional sterility from the buildings.[12] Learning centers, commonly referred to as "instructional materials centers," will combine audio-visual materials with all types of conventional library materials. Libraries are being designed with private and semi-private study booths or carrels to encourage individual research on the part of pupils. As the philosophy of placing more responsibility on the student for his own learning gains wider acceptance, individualized learning facilities will become more common. Recent findings in human growth and psychology tend to substantiate the need for the pupils to assume more responsibility for their own learning process. Future curriculums will be designed with these data in mind.

The large amount of audio-visual learning today's children do by way of television, before they ever come to school, has had a strong effect on the amount of usage of the same kind of machines within the school. Textbooks that are used by today's pupils have little resemblance to those of twenty years ago. Illustrations and word pictures, puzzles, mathematical games, and completion questions utilize the visual approach to learning. How else can a society hope to educate its children who in early childhood have been thoroughly conditioned to an audio-visual approach to learning?

Ever increasing enrollments, at all levels of education, have put great pressure on schools in favor of groupings of pupils and will continue to exert such pressure in the years ahead. Both the elementary and secondary schools have re-examined their methods of grouping pupils. Ability groupings, interest groupings, large- and small-group teaching situations, and team teaching are some of the solutions that have been tried. New arrangements of teaching talent and interests, along with the use of more automated instructional devices, seem

[12]Educational Facilities Laboratories, Inc., *The Cost of a Schoolhouse* (New York: International Press, 1960), pp. 132–133.

to offer at least a partial solution to the population pressures. A recent study by the National Association of Secondary School Principals, concerned with utilization of staff in the secondary schools, supports more efficient use of teachers as members of teaching teams and in large- and small-group teaching situations.[13]

One of the most potent forces affecting our public schools in the last fifty years is the deliberate move toward desegregation of public education. As Americans we have long believed, at the idea level, in "equality for all men," even though we have not practiced it in many of our social and cultural institutions. With the historic Supreme Court decision of May 17, 1954, public schools were faced with a task of major social and educational magnitude. Progress has been made in this area in many sections of the country. Virtually all of the states that were completely segregated prior to 1954 have moved to at least token integration. However, as late as 1961, it was estimated that in the 17 states and the District of Columbia where segregation was accepted as public policy, less than 9.3 per cent of the Negro children were attending integrated schools.[14] This task is far from being completed and will concern the schools for many years to come. Although the Supreme Court decision has helped immeasurably to begin the process, it is just a beginning. To legislate social change that is deeply rooted in tradition, historical convention, and local practice is almost impossible. Social change takes time, experimentation, emotional involvement, evaluation, experience, and acceptance by a new generation.

Representative examples of current social, industrial, technological, international, and scientific forces affecting curriculum building have been given. Let's take a look now at where we stand, currently, with reference to our public schools and the curriculum building tasks they face in the immediate future. How much curriculum experimentation is going on in our schools? To what extent

[13]National Association of Secondary-School Principals, *New Directions to Quality Education: The Secondary School Tomorrow* (Washington: The Association, 1960).

[14]Jim Leesan, "The First Ten Years," *Phi Delta Kappan*, XLV (May 1964), 385.

is the total school involved in such experimentation? How deeply is the average school able to be involved in curriculum building and experimentation?

OUR SCHOOLS TODAY: THE FEW AND THE MANY

Many public schools throughout the nation are experimenting, on a very limited basis, with changes in curriculum. Few schools are deeply and totally involved in curricular experimentation. Generally speaking, the traditional reasons given for lack of serious involvement in curricular change are: lack of leadership, lack of time, budgetary limitations, community attitudes toward teachers and the school, and lack of instructional materials. There are several other factors that also contribute to the lack of curricular experimentation, and these will be discussed individually in later chapters.

Educators are usually cautious about curriculum change. They tend to accept what is already respected and what has already been tried and proved by other teachers' experience. They have not been, for the most part, a group of professional persons who were willing to gamble and risk failure; instead, they have been satisfied to maintain the status quo. There are many good reasons for this. One of the most perceptive explanations is offered by Brickell, in a recent study of schools in the State of New York.

A school, like any other institution, tends to continue doing what it was established to do, holding itself relatively stable and resisting attempts at restructuring. There is a sound reason for this: Stability in the institutional structure makes for maximum output of the results that structure was designed to produce. Any change in the arrangement of its elements tends to cut down production, at least until new habit patterns are formed.[15]

Those who teach face a dilemma in the light of present pressures for new design and new results: first, they must maintain stability, and, second, they must attempt to change their patterns of instruc-

[15]Henry M. Brickell, *Organizing New York State for Educational Change* (Albany, New York: State Department of Education, 1961), p. 19.

tion. One of these tasks at a time is normally sufficient to occupy most teachers; hence, the slow pace of change. One concept seems to be quite clear in relation to change in curriculum. On the basis of considerable evidence from research, it seems apparent that we may have to look at the problem of creating curriculum change from a new perspective. The traditional role of the public school as an institution may need modifications and some reshaping of its structural elements.

There are several possible ways of approaching this problem. One method would be a re-examination of the role of the school in its own community. This method would have to involve clear communication and working with all the elements of a community: social, political, governmental, educational, business, industrial, and religious. The schools could be carefully evaluated to see if they were adequately meeting the needs of the local community and its youth. This kind of approach might well bring a realization to many communities that a horse-and-buggy curriculum is attempting to pull a jet-age pupil population.

Another possible approach to a new perspective on the need for instructional change would be a careful study by school personnel of the objectives of their educational program from kindergarten through the high-school or community-college level. Attempting a thorough examination and study of objectives may well show the necessity for better articulation of programs of studies. There is a pressing need for continuity of educational experiences. School personnel need to be aware of relationships in learning experiences in order that they may show pupils how the work of the seventh grade, for instance, is directly related to some earlier experiences of their fifth-grade year and also related to what they will study in the tenth grade. When pupils begin to see purpose and relationships in learning, they are far more inclined to be receptive to new ideas. Too much of our educational experience today is of a disjointed nature, and this very lack of continuity is one deterrent to pupil effort.

A third possible approach to this problem would be through a study of the purposes of education. What are the reasons we educate our youth today in the way we do? What seem to be the major purposes in providing for individual growth? What are the purposes of education that are relative to and necessary for our society and its needs? Are the purposes for the individual and society compatible? Where are the points at which we can combine individual and societal needs and encompass the growth of both within the same framework? How much unnecessary duplication of effort is contained in our present curriculums? Do homogeneous groupings by ability and interest aid in accomplishing our basic purposes or do they deter us? Is it possible that pupils can assist us in formulating some of the purposes of our curriculums? Must all of our programs be entirely conceived and executed by the adults, or should pupils offer some ideas of educational values that are important to them? Close examination of our basic purposes may give us a new perspective on the task before us.

A final suggested approach (and perhaps this should be the starting point rather than the final suggestion) would be a long, hard look at what an education really involves for an individual. In the evolution of curriculum, from a relatively slow pace in 1920 to the hurried, harried pace of the sixties in America, we have had little time to consider this basic question. Much of the recent emphasis in public education has been on increasing uniformity rather than on encouraging diversity. The nonconformist has a rough road to follow in our present educational institutions, for the median seems to be conformity to a norm. The process of becoming educated tends to become lost in the competition for grade-point averages. Whether a pupil learns anything of real value or not has little bearing on his completion of a specific level of schooling, so long as he maintains an acceptable average.

Some of our institutions have been justly accused of offering a cafeteria type of education, where the pupil selects his menu to such a large extent that he often has an extremely unbalanced educational diet. In other cases, the diet is so rigidly prescribed that it cannot hope to begin to meet the educational needs of the diverse pupils being served. Do we want a supermarket type of education on a serve-yourself basis, or do we want an education so tightly structured that it offers little room for exploration? Probably neither extreme represents the most desirable type of curriculum.

In reference to the question, "What is an education?" we need to make some fundamental changes in our thinking if we wish to serve this generation and the coming ones adequately. Is an education supposed to give an individual all the answers, information, and necessary ways of procedure so that he stops learning when he graduates from school? In a very real sense, it would seem that the legitimate purpose of educating an individual should be to equip him with an unending thirst for knowledge and an active willingness to spend a lifetime questioning and searching for answers. An education should prepare the individual to begin, with the help and training of school experiences, a life of active searching for better solutions to his own and society's problems. Is this the kind of mental outlook that our schools presently engender in their graduates? What would the format of a curriculum be that would promote such an outlook for its graduates? How could such a curriculum be built? Who would be involved in building a curriculum with such a goal? What trends in curriculum building are currently being tried that aim toward this goal? The remaining chapters of this book will examine possible answers to such questions. Our examination of curriculum will consider operational methods, the roles of concerned parties, forces currently operative in our society, research studies, and techniques for creating a more functional, attractive design for learning.

SUGGESTED READINGS

Association for Supervision and Curriculum Development. *Action for Curriculum Improvement.* Washington: The Association, 1951.
————. *A Look at Continuity in the School Program.* Washington: The Association, 1958.
————. *Balance in the Curriculum.* Washington: The Association, 1961.
————. *Creating a Good Environment for Learning.* Washington: The Association, 1954.
————. *Leadership for Improving Instruction.* Washington: The Association, 1960.
————. *Perceiving, Behaving, Becoming: A New Focus for Education.* Washington: The Association, 1962.
————. *What Are the Sources of Curriculum?* Washington: The Association, 1962.

Beauchamp, George A. *Planning the Elementary School Curriculum.* Boston: Allyn and Bacon, Inc., 1956.

Breslow, Alice, *et al.* "Forces Influencing Curriculum," *Review of Educational Research,* 30 (June 1960), 199–225.

Combs, Arthur, and Snygg, D. *Individual Behavior: A Perceptual Approach to Behavior.* New York: Harper & Brothers, 1959.

Gwynn, J. Minor. *Curriculum Principles and Social Trends.* 3rd ed. New York: The Macmillan Co., 1960.

Havighurst, Robert J. *Human Development and Education.* New York: Longmans, Green and Co., 1953.

National Association of Secondary School Principals Association. *New Directions to Quality Education: The Secondary School Tomorrow.* Washington: The Association, 1960.

Thelen, Herbert A. *Education and the Human Quest.* New York: Harper & Brothers, 1960.

The Work of the Curriculum Coordinator in Selected New Jersey Schools. New York: Bureau of Publications, Teachers College, Columbia University, 1955.

Wiles, Kimball. *The Changing Curriculum of the American High School.* Englewood Cliffs, N. J.: Prentice-Hall, Inc., 1963.

II

WHO BUILDS THE CURRICULUM?

Traditionally, in America, public education has been a matter of state function and local control. It is therefore quite logical that the individual state has been a primary force in shaping the schools' curriculums. The major arm of state government charged with the responsibility of supporting and maintaining the public school system is the state department of education.

THE ROLE OF THE STATE
DEPARTMENT OF EDUCATION

The state superintendent of public instruction is the chief administrative officer of the state department of education and, in most cases, is an elected public official. His appointed staff consists of administrative assistants, finance and transportation officers, supervisory staff in special subject-matter areas or levels of public education, and a large body of clerical personnel. Certification of all teachers, administrators, and supervisory personnel is usually handled by a special branch of the state department of education, known as the certification division. This entails a heavy burden of responsibility of a highly complicated nature, as this division renders service to all public-school institutional personnel.

Another vital service offered by state departments of education is directly concerned with curriculum and is normally personified in the office of the state coordinator of curriculum. A state coordinator of curriculum is the person who gives leadership, on a state-wide basis, to the area of curriculum development, including planning and evaluation of new programs. He is also the person who supplies the motivation for and leadership of state-wide committees appointed to produce new curriculum publications. Another major function fulfilled by the person in this office is planning state-wide meetings, sectional meetings and workshops where teachers and administrators get together to discuss and share new ideas.

There is a definite administrative hierarchy in public education. The man at the top of the hierarchial ladder is the state superintendent. Local superintendents and principals pay close attention to any and all communications from the state superintendent, for he represents the major source of financial support for public schools.

In many instances, state departments of education have too small a staff to be really effective on the local level. The basic philosophy behind the operational procedures of most state departments, however, is a maximum of encouragement of local leadership and a minimum of state control. The responsibilities given to state departments are generally greater than they are able to fulfill with their limited staffs; hence, the sectional meetings and workshops, where state department personnel try to keep in touch with the largest possible number of local educators.

Since state departments of education do operate by encouraging local leadership and exerting a minimum of state control, one might well take a look at some of the definite obligations that they have regarding curriculum at the local level. The major function of the state department of education, in relation to curriculum, is to enforce the legislative intent of state laws in reference to the "common schools." In the course of fulfilling this obligation, the basic core of local curriculum is established. Most state departments of education have general responsibility for the minimum courses of study offered and the direction of the administration and supervision of all schools supported by public taxation. These schools generally include all levels from kindergarten through grades 12 or 14. Grades 13 and 14 represent the development of community colleges or public junior colleges, which have been incorporated in some states as a part of the public-school program.

In most instances, the state department also has some responsibility for approval of curriculums being offered for teacher education by the colleges and universities within the state. Realistically, the state departments exert a very strong influence on teacher education, since the division of certification establishes the requirements for approval to teach. Both state-supported and privately-endowed colleges and universities must tailor their curriculums to meet state requirements in order that their graduates will be prepared for certification. In some states, the actual development of specific courses for pre-service teacher education is left to the discretion of the college, and only the broad areas of study are outlined by state authorities. The trend in certifying teachers is to require "institutional recommendation," by a college administrator such as a dean or department head, in addition to completion of prescribed courses.

What kinds of prescriptions do the state departments give to local school authorities in relation to specific courses of study? In the elementary school, instruction is required in language arts (reading, literature, spelling, handwriting, and oral and written expression), arithmetic, American history, geography, science, health, physical education, art, and music.[1] Any additions to the curriculum usually come from local promptings; a specific example is foreign language in the elementary school.

On the secondary-school level, course requirements are usually determined by graduation requirements and these, in turn, are closely related to college-entrance requirements. Graduation requirements in most states consist of the following subjects:

English	3-4 years
American History	1 year
State History	1 year
Civics	1 year
½-3 social studies units in additional to above requirements	

½-3 social studies units in
addition to above requirements

---

[1]Howard H. Cummings and Helen K. Mackintosh, *Curriculum Responsibilities of State Departments of Education* (Washington: U. S. Department of Health, Education, and Welfare, 1958), p. 8. See entire bulletin for detailed description of study of all facets of state department of education resonsibilities regarding curriculum.

Mathematics	1 year or more
Science	1 year or more (usually general science and biology)
Health	½-2 units
Physical Education	4 units (driver education is required in some states and given up to 1 unit of credit)

In addition to those listed, other subjects are frequently required. Those most frequently required are industrial arts for boys and home economics for girls, and art and music.[2] Other courses are generally recommended but *not* required, with the exception of alcohol education, which 31 states do require. Most of the "recommended" courses for high schools fall in the relatively new curriculum areas, and their content and methods of instruction are usually left to local authorities.[3] A sampling of "recommended" courses would include the following: air-age education, atomic energy, conservation, home and family living, driver education, human relations, mental hygiene, moral and spiritual values, narcotics, safety, sex education, and work experience. Practically all high schools also offer elective courses, for which Carnegie Unit credit (page 28) may be earned, such as speech, drama, foreign language, chemistry, physics, earth science, business education, agriculture and diversified occupations.

In examining the curriculum of the secondary schools, it is apparent that state requirements largely determine the number of courses that a secondary school may offer. Most secondary schools operate on a six- to eight-period school day with the final period reserved for activities or conferences. When a secondary school pupil's schedule is set up to include all the required subjects, little time is left for exploration of other areas of study. This is one reason some schools have moved to an eight-period school day. Lack of time for enrichment has also led some secondary schools to the "module concept."

The module concept of class scheduling is based on a standard unit of time that can be doubled or tripled as the learning activity requires. For instance, instead of the normal seven- or eight-period

[2]*Ibid.*, p. 8.
[3]*Ibid.*, p. 13.

day of most secondary schools, with each period 45–50 minutes, the module concept puts variety into the schedule. The module may be set by the school at 20–25 minutes in length. Large group presentations are normally one module long. Small group-discussion classes, however, are always at least two or three modules long to allow time to explore issues and to clarify pertinent points. Classes in home economics and industrial arts are also longer—three or four modules —to provide time for work on projects. Although this system does present some scheduling problems, usually they can be worked out. The basic idea upon which it rests is to suit the length of the class period to the needs of the specific learning activity. Breaking up the traditional uniform length of class time may be a first step in bringing needed curriculum change to the secondary school. Lakeview High in Decatur, Evanston Township High in Evanston, and Ridgewood High in Norridge are three examples of Illinois high schools currently operating under this system.

THE CARNEGIE UNIT—AN INHIBITOR OF CHANGE

The use of the Carnegie Unit as a quantitative measure of secondary-school study began with the report issued by the Carnegie Foundation early in this century, where a unit was defined as ". . . being a course of five periods weekly throughout an academic year."[4] From that time to the present, mainly to aid in the simplification of academic bookkeeping, the Carnegie Unit has been the standard measure for secondary-school credit.

As Smith, Stanley, and Shores point out, the assumptions underlying the general adoption of the Carnegie Unit have never been validated.

The system has been accepted, not because of its demonstrated educational advantages, but because its theory of equivalent units makes it extremely convenient in academic bookkeeping. No one knows the length of class period, nor the frequency of periods,

[4]Carnegie Foundation for the Advancement of Teaching, *Annual Report of the President and Treasurer*, 1906, p. 38.

most conducive to learning in a given content course. It may be that just as much could be attained by reducing the time devoted to various subjects and distributing the time thus allotted in new ways not now found in practice. Could just as much American history be learned in three class meetings per week as in five per week? Could it be that more learning would result from two American history classes a week for a year than five classes a week for a semester? Is it reasonable to suppose that the attitude of dependency in intellectual matters, so often found in students, is due in part to the frequency of class meetings and the consequent tendency of teachers to carry the responsibilities of the class?[5]

The questions asked by Smith, Stanley, and Shores in 1950 have been investigated and their suggestions are being tried in some secondary schools. These schools are experimenting with the recommendations of the National Association of Secondary Schools Principal's study of Utilization of the Staff in the Secondary School. The recommendations of this study, which was financed by the Ford Foundation, are commonly referred to as the "Trump Plan," after Dr. J. Lloyd Trump, associate secretary of N.A.S.S.P. and director of the commission that produced the study. Recommendations include utilizing large- and small-group instruction, varying the size of large groups with the type of instruction, and varying the amount of time according to subjects, at different stages within a subject, and in accordance with student maturity. The study also recommended that students should be scheduled for independent study on an average of twelve hours out of the usual thirty-hour school week. These recommendations, based on research and experimentation in more than one hundred high schools, began to answer the questions asked by Smith, Stanley, and Shores. New arrangements of time patterns and staff patterns are beginning to emerge in our secondary schools as we move toward increasing the responsibility of the learner for the education he is to receive.[6]

[5]B. Othanel Smith, William O. Stanley, and J. Harlan Shores, *Fundamentals of Curriculum Development* (New York: World Book Company, 1950), pp. 364–365.

[6]J. Lloyd Trump, *New Directions to Quality Education: The Secondary School Tomorrow* (Washington: N.A.S.S.P., 1960).

LOCAL ADMINISTRATORS AND CURRICULUM BUILDING

On the local levels, much can be done by administrators and their staffs in conjunction with the teachers to build better curriculums. Although the state sets the framework and draws the guidelines for curriculum, much of the actual implementation is left for local school personnel. Almost all of the "extras" and areas of exploration in any curriculum are a result of local influences. The greatest amount of power to change and improve the curriculum lies in the hand of local administrators.[7] Brickell's study of the dynamics of instructional change in the elementary and secondary schools of New York State has amply documented this statement.

In the past, we have been inclined to believe that classroom teachers were the most powerful change agents in curriculum; but this idea seems to be more theory than practice. The classic study by Mort and Cornell supports the same kind of findings as the Brickell study. Mort and Cornell found that administrators were the vital factor in the initiation of change, placing first among involved persons in providing leadership in schools that had made changes. In other schools, neutrality on the part of the principals prevented changes. It was also found, in some instances, that administrative patterns and policies prevented program development.[8]

On the basis of the findings presented above, one concludes that curriculum building must be initiated and implemented by administrators. This appears to be the most promising method of actually changing the school program. For the most part, the administrators of the past have been bogged down in the minutiae of record keeping and office routine, and the programs of educational administration that trained administrators were "thing-centered" or "task-centered," not staff and curriculum-centered.

An encouraging innovation is the sixth-year graduate program in educational administration, an attempt to professionalize this vital

[7]Brickell, *Organizing New York State.*
[8]Paul R. Mort and F. G. Cornell, *American Schools in Transition* (New York: Bureau of Publications, Teachers College, Columbia University, 1941).

work through study designed specifically for public-school administrators. Available at many institutions of higher learning throughout the nation, these graduate programs are being vigorously encouraged by the administrators' national professional organization, the
American Association of School Administrators. Centers for research in educational administration have contributed greatly to a
beginning science of school administration. The W. W. Kellogg
Foundation has financed numerous research studies under university
direction throughout the nation. The new graduate programs should
give rise to administrators whose emphases will be upon program,
staff, public relations, and all the interactions taking place in the
operation of a public school. Utilization of this knowledge and experience should improve curriculums and human relationships
within the school and community.

Most of the lack of major structural change in curriculum practices by classroom teachers is the result of the administrative hierarchy. Only within the confines of the classroom is the teacher a
free agent, and the changes he can make without administrative support are minor ones.[9] Public-school administration operates on the
line- and staff-principle of organization, and the teacher occupies a
subservient position to the administrative group. Fear of administrative disapproval or retaliation has often kept the classroom teacher
from even trying to change his course content, methods, or philo-
sophical approach to teaching. Each year our public-school teachers
become better educated and trained, and as they improve their professional competence they should have more security in approaching their administrators to suggest curriculum changes.

There is one basic truth concerning curriculum building that has
been well documented in numerous works in this field: the idea that
curriculum must be adapted to local needs. Although a plan for
curriculum improvement may be borrowed from a neighboring
community, it must be tailored to meet local needs. It is most important, when attempting to introduce basic changes in instructional
procedures, that administrators obtain help for their teachers in
learning how to work with the new procedure and how to make any

[9]Brickell, *Organizing New York State*, pp. 24-26.

changes necessary for the particular community. Classroom teachers are understandably reticent to try something new if they feel inadequately prepared to teach it. More new programs fail because of the classroom teacher's inability to handle the material than from any basic resentment teachers may have toward change.[10]

Administrators at the local level often introduce new courses at the insistence of the public. Parental pressure, if aroused, acts as a goad to local administrators and is usually not withdrawn until the recommended change has been made. Criticisms of the teaching of reading is an example of pressure put on administrators. Because of public pressure, many elementary schools have returned to the old phonetic approach to teaching reading, although it is often used along with word recognition or other approaches. Another area of public concern in recent years (although much work was done by the educators thirty-forty years ago) has been the provision of a program for gifted children. With the renewed emphasis upon the need for scientists, the public clamored for special opportunities for the gifted. Administrators have generally been quick to accept the challenge and have included advanced courses and enrichment for superior students.

At the other end of the scale, American public schools over the past twenty-five years have greatly improved curriculums and facilities for educating the physically and/or emotionally handicapped child. Numerous school systems have developed programs for children who need a special teacher, a special curriculum, and special physical facilities. Diagnostic and remedial centers for these children have been established in most parts of the nation. State facilities have been made available to rural school systems, and colleges and universities have cooperated with local school systems and invited use of their professional staff and facilities to help with these children. This kind of cooperative effort represents a fine start on the road to even closer cooperation between public schools and the institutions of higher learning that train and educate the teachers for the public schools.

[10]*Ibid.*, pp. 30–33.

COOPERATION NEEDED
BETWEEN COLLEGES AND PUBLIC SCHOOLS

One important way to effect change in curriculum could be through joint efforts of college and public-school personnel. Unfortunately, in the past, there has been a very wide gap between college staffs and public-school personnel. College staffs were often accused by public-school personnel of being too highly theoretical, and the accusation was often justly made. College teachers need to visit public-school classrooms, especially those who teach specific subject matter to potential teachers.

On a college campus, far from the battle line of the public-school classroom, a professor may tend to become a bit idealistic and unrealistic. After a visit to a public-school classroom, the same professor is usually inclined to be more objective and realistic. Our public schools do attempt to educate "all the children of all the people," and this group represents a much wider range of interests, abilities, and backgrounds than most colleges have in the students on their campuses. If a college instructor has had no contact with public schools since his own experience as a pupil, one could hardly expect him to be cognizant of today's problems in public education.

An excellent example of cooperative curriculum planning is described in a publication of the University of Toronto Press.[11] It describes the curriculum studies in English, social science, and science that were made by the Board of Education of the Toronto public-school system and by members of the staff of the University of Toronto who are involved in the preparation of teachers. Representative committees containing public-school teachers and administrators and university personnel worked with the problem of curriculum revision in the public schools of Toronto. This joint effort brought entirely new outlooks to both the university and public-school personnel.

[11]Northrop Frye (ed.), *Design For Learning* (Toronto: University of Toronto Press, 1962), p. 4 ff.

In Toronto geographic proximity makes such an arrangement easy since the university is located in the same city as the public-school system. In order that our public-school curriculums may be modernized and updated to keep pace with the rapid advances in the many fields of knowledge today, more cooperative curriculum building of this type is necessary here in our own country. Cooperative programs could be established on an area or regional basis, and some of the time now allotted to institutes, workshops, and other in-service educational programs could be allotted to such projects. College and university personnel should recognize that they would work on joint curriculum-planning committees as contributing members, rather than consultants, their traditional role in the past.

An example of cooperative curriculum planning of a different nature, in a specific field of study, that of science, is described in Bruner's *The Process of Education.*[12] In 1959, under the auspices of the National Academy of Science, a conference at Woods Hole, Massachusetts, brought together some of the nation's outstanding authorities in biology, professional education, mathematics, history, psychology, physics, classics, medicine, and cinematography. The conference was centered around an over-all appraisal of ways to improve science education in elementary and secondary schools. The Woods Hole conference and the insights gained from cooperative planning led to the publication of the book by Jerome Bruner, who served as chairman of the conference. Prior to the conference, studies by the School Mathematics Study Group, the University of Illinois Committee on School Mathematics, the Chemical Bond Approach Project, and the Physical Science Study Committee in Physics provided the groundwork for this over-all appraisal of science education in the public schools.

Although almost all of the participants in the Woods Hole conference were university or industrial personnel, this type of conference at least gives an interdisciplinary approach to cooperative planning that represents a welcome breaking down of barriers between isolated subject-matter disciplines. This type of conference is a

[12]Jerome S. Bruner, *The Process of Education* (Cambridge: Harvard University Press, 1960).

step in the right direction and could lead to working arrangements like the Toronto experiment between university and public-school personnel.

Perhaps the greatest single problem of curriculum building is the lack of continuity of learning experiences throughout the school life of the pupil. The lack of articulation of program is not confined to the elementary and secondary schools but extends into the college level. With rare exceptions, there is little real articulation between high school and college. A reasonable approach to a solution of this problem is to establish closer working relationships between college and public-school personnel.

TEACHER EDUCATION AS A FACTOR IN CURRICULUM

Subject matter is important; no one would question this. Yet, in the preparation of teachers, colleges and universities must be aware of the necessity for classroom teachers to deal with individual differences of children. These differences appear in spite of attempts to group children homogeneously by achievement and intelligence scores. Such criteria are used in most schools to group pupils, not because they are the best but because they are easily obtainable and easily standardized. Colleges and universities that train public-school teachers also help to provide the foundation for future curriculum building, since "teachers tend to teach as they have been taught." In a discussion of the controversy that has raged concerning the proper education of teachers, the following insight is offered by Sarason, Davidson, and Blatt:

If teaching were viewed primarily as the feeding of information and knowledge to children, and this is too frequently the case at all levels of schooling, the nature of individual differences would be a less thorny problem. But, because everyone is apparently agreed that the important aim is to enable children to utilize and act upon (that is, think about) knowledge in ways which expand intellectual skills, at the same time that curiosity about ideas and problems is strengthened, then the nature and range of individual differences become crucial. Not all children can be motivated in one particular way, not all children attack problems in similar ways (not all scientists go about research in the same style), not all children are equally curious, and not all children with the same test scores learn at the same pace or in the same ways. The ability to recognize and cope with such individual differences is, unfortunately, not highly related to the degree of background in the liberal arts and sciences.[13]

Since teachers are necessarily concerned as curriculum builders—a very vital portion of their instructional role—one may hope that all teacher-training institutions will work toward a better balance between subject matter per se and professional education course work.

SOME POSSIBLE REMEDIES FOR EXISTING PROBLEMS

Public education is one of the biggest businesses currently in operation on the American scene. With curriculum the major concern of many persons professionally and privately interested in our schools, it would seem logical to recommend the employment of a curriculum coordinator or director for every school system. Although some systems do employ such professional personnel, their number is relatively few. In some systems this function is performed by an assistant superintendent. It makes little difference what administrative title goes with the job, but it makes a world of difference whether or not this extremely important job is given the full attention it demands. Professionally competent leadership is the most necessary ingredient for successful curriculum building.

The major problem of lack of articulation in curriculums could be attacked on the local level if teachers and administrators were given some "released time" from normal duties. One free afternoon a month could do wonders for improved curriculums. For many years, teachers have been expected to improve themselves and their curriculums after four o'clock in the afternoon. Realistically, after

[13]Seymour B. Sarason, Kenneth Davidson, and Burton Blatt, *The Preparation of Teachers: An Unstudied Problem in Education* (New York: John Wiley and Sons, Inc., 1962), pp. 33–34.

four o'clock there is little if any energy left to be used for constructive or creative purposes. Some communities do free school personnel for these purposes, on occasion, and thousands more could do so if the school board were approached with a planned in-service program of curriculum study.

Communication is at the heart of the problem of nonarticulation in most school communities, just as it is the core of a host of predicaments in business, government, and international relations. At least, in most school systems, administrators and teachers speak the same language, so the problem might be solved if time were made available and the leadership could be secured.

Certainly, better communication between state and local personnel would help to improve local curriculums. Although most state offices function as well as can be expected within the limits of budgets and staff, more area workshops and conferences, under the leadership of local personnel with the consultant service of the state department, would be helpful.

A new method of assessing the worth of secondary-school learning experiences, which will show more evidence of depth and breadth than the Carnegie Unit, is needed. From experiments with the Trump Plan in selected secondary schools may come a better method of academic bookkeeping that will honor what we know about learning and also illustrate through transcripts exactly where the emphasis has been in the pupil's study. Such a method may well involve considerably more descriptive material, but should be infinitely more valuable to those persons who read transcripts and try to evaluate quality and depth of secondary-school curriculums.

Programs of professional leadership training providing additional information in administrative skills and a general broadening of academic backgrounds of potential administrators and those currently engaged in public-school administration hold great promise. Graduate programs for educational administrators are rapidly moving away from the managerial emphasis and are emphasizing staff and personnel relationships and the role of the administrator as a competent, inspiring educational leader. One of the most common clichés among classroom teachers has been, "As the principal goes, so goes the school." This cliché may be extended to include the top local administrative officer, the superintendent, and from this point, right up the hierarchial ladder to the state superintendent. The demand today is for competent professional leadership, and the institutions of higher learning throughout the nation are intensely involved in creating ways and means to meet this need.

Closer working relationships between public schools and the institutions of higher learning that prepare their teachers are just around the proverbial corner. Artificial walls that have traditionally separated public schools and colleges are beginning to crack and crumble. Such progress brings greater potential articulation and insight as the reward to both levels of education. Active participation by college personnel with public-school personnel should bring about enriched curriculum planning and building programs from which the pupils should reap great benefits.

Curriculum building by so many different parties makes for a rather perplexing process, as the reader has no doubt gathered at this stage of the book. It is a highly complicated, involved task that demands energetic leadership, coordination, and constant attention. The following three chapters will be directed at delineation of the roles of administrators, classroom teachers, and parents and pupils, as they individually and jointly work together at the task of building better curriculums.

SUGGESTED READINGS

Brickell, Henry M. *Organizing New York State for Educational Change.* Albany: State Department of Education, 1961.

Bruner, Jerome S. *The Process of Education.* Cambridge: Harvard University Press, 1960.

Cummings, Howard H., and Mackintosh, Helen K. *Curriculum Responsibilities of State Departments of Education.* Washington: U.S. Department of Health, Education, and Welfare, 1958.

Frye, Northrop, ed. *Design for Learning.* Toronto: University of Toronto Press, 1962.

Krug, Edward A. *Curriculum Planning.* New York: Harper & Brothers, 1957.

Menge, J. Wilmer, and Faunce, Roland C. *Working Together for Better Schools.* New York: American Book Company, 1953.

Miel, Alice. *Changing the Curriculum: A Social Process.* New York: D. Appleton-Century Co., Inc., 1946.

Mort, Paul R., and Cornell, F. G. *American Schools in Transition.* New York: Bureau of Publications, Teachers College, Columbia University, 1941.

Saylor, J. Galen, and Alexander, William M. *Curriculum Planning for Better Teaching and Learning.* New York: Rinehart and Company, Inc., 1954.

Smith, B. O., *et al. Fundamentals of Curriculum Development.* New York: World Book Company, 1950.

Spears, Harold. *Curriculum Planning Through In-Service Programs.* Englewood Cliffs, N.J.: Prentice-Hall, Inc., 1957.

Taba, Hilda. *Curriculum Development: Theory and Practice.* New York: Harcourt, Brace, and World, Inc., 1962.

III

THE ADMINISTRATOR'S ROLE IN CURRICULUM BUILDING

If you were in a military unit and wished permission for a method of operation that was slightly different from that called for in the appropriate manual, to whom would you go? The obvious answer is your immediate superior officer. So it is in public schools, when any change in curriculum will involve more than the one teacher in the confines of a single classroom. A new method of operation that involves only one teacher and one classroom is seldom questioned by administrators. As a matter of fact, many administrators are not even aware of such a change. On the other hand, when a curriculum change by a teacher will involve other teachers, permission must be obtained.

Normally, the administrator concerned is the building principal, who, in turn, is directly responsible to the system superintendent. Usually the principal feels compelled to discuss proposed changes with his superintendent and obtain higher administrative permission from him. Before the classroom teacher may make a curriculum change involving others on the staff, the administrators must be convinced that the proposed new method or content offers potentially better learning experiences for the pupils.

The administrator, then, stands in the most crucial position of all in regard to curriculum change within his school system. Encouragement for teachers who wish to experiment in the classroom is the greatest gift an administrator may bestow upon his staff. Creating an atmosphere in his school that makes teachers feel like professional equals whose opinions are sought and welcomed will do much to promote better curriculum building. Many teachers, as professionals, are persons who like to try new approaches to their particular tasks. These persons will work harder and longer, with better results for their efforts, if the administrator gives them a flexible set of ground rules. Without minimizing the worth or necessity of curriculum guides, we should nevertheless put the horse before the cart, in order to utilize creative thinking and talent more efficiently. Professional personnel in the schools always pull the "curriculum cart." Why not make it possible for them to participate at the decision-making level and help decide the style and design of their cart and its content?

For every school administrator who attempts to free his teaching staff to think and act creatively, there is one who inhibits and suppresses his teachers. What are the reasons for this? In American public education, school administrators have been consistently forced, in all but the large metropolitan centers, to work with teachers who lack proper training and certification; inadequately prepared teachers are still too plentiful. Lack of adequate salary schedules for teachers to compensate for the rising costs of living is also a major factor. Below the surface, but of compelling importance, lies the value system of the American people in regard to the teacher and education itself. When a society does not place education at the pinnacle of its value system, all kinds of problems are created in its schools. One of the chief ones is economic: The administrator must hire less qualified teachers with the limited monies available. With weak staff members, an administrator usually feels compelled to rule with a heavy hand for the benefit of the pupils.

A major portion of the school administrator's role is interpreting the curriculum to the community. In order to perform this vital task successfully, the administrator needs to be an educator first and an organizer and manager second. Unfortunately, and often by necessity, these characteristics are found in reverse order. However, the concept that administration is primarily managerial technique seems to have outlived its usefulness, particularly in public education. Although managerial techniques are still necessary, the emphasis in the training of administrators must be changed. First, the administrator must be able to provide educational leadership for his community, staff, and teaching personnel. Secondly, he must be able to perform all the minute, detailed tasks of managing a complex business operation.

A new breed of public-school administrator is in the making as this book is being written. It is this new kind of administrator that will be discussed in this chapter. As we look ahead, the whole tone of public-school administration would appear to be different from what it has traditionally been. Our emphasis needs to be placed on the future, for this new group of administrators will be the group who will most strongly affect curriculum building. They will affect it dynamically, for their whole educational training program is a dynamic one that places its emphasis upon the leadership characteristics of school administration and the understanding and use of educational research. Although the new public-school administrator learns competency in areas such as school law, school finance, transportation, and so forth, major emphasis is given to his role as instructional leader of a school system. As an instructional leader, the public-school administrator sits in the most significant position in regard to curriculum change.

People who set out to produce change are bound up in the process themselves. In order for curriculum to change, people must change. Teachers must work in new dimensions; administrators must work in new ways with each other and with teachers. In the process of trying to create a better program, administrators and teachers must create new roles for themselves. They will need to see themselves differently and to behave differently with pupils.

PRINCIPAL'S ROLE IN CURRICULUM BUILDING

Pritzkau, in describing the importance of a school principal to successful development, makes the following statement:

Most successful curriculum improvement programs have their start in the local school unit. Within this local unit, the program must have its initial beginnings in a setting of familiarity for the teachers, the classrooms. Teachers are inclined to look instinctively to the principal for leadership and encouragement in such undertakings. Of all the persons in the school, the principal is the one in a key position to provide the conditions necessary for these beginnings of curriculum development.[1]

Teachers do look to principals for leadership as they attempt something new, be it introducing new content or trying new methods. In either case, the principal is the one to whom the classroom teacher turns for support. Moving from the known to the unknown has provided the pathway for scientists to enter the world of space travel. Why shouldn't teachers use the same exciting roadway to better teaching? Many teachers can and will do so, if administrators will give them the opportunity and support necessary for experimentation.

A doctoral research study, by the writer, investigated administrator-teacher relationships as one of several factors inhibiting curriculum development. One of the sub-hypotheses of the study stated the problem in the following manner:

If teachers feel that they are not included by their administrators in planning and policy-making decisions which affect school operation, this situation will be interpreted by them as a barrier to curriculum improvement.[2]

From the conclusions of the study, under the heading of "Implications for Curriculum Workers," comes this suggestion:

Curriculum workers have the opportunity to work with principals and teachers. In this dual role, a curriculum worker may be able to do a great deal in furthering better understandings between teachers and principals. Many chances are available to set up work groups which include the principals as well as the teachers. Opportunities can be created in a curriculum-improvement program for joint decision-making experiences by teachers and principals. Principals can be encouraged to share decisions about daily school routine with teacher committees, so that teachers will always feel

[1]P. T. Pritzkau, *Dynamics of Curriculum Improvement* (Englewood Cliffs, N. J.: Prentice-Hall, Inc., 1959), pp. 104–105.

[2]Donald F. Cay, "Selected Teachers' Expressed Judgments Concerning Barriers to Curriculum Improvement" (Unpublished doctoral dissertation, University of Florida, 1960), p. 9.

that their interest is being represented. Better relationships between teachers and principals can be fostered by curriculum workers in the course of their work, and as better relationships grow, teachers will be more encouraged to participate in curriculum-improvement activities.[3]

The term "curriculum worker," as used in this book, means any person in an administrative capacity or consultant role who works with members of a school system to improve curriculum. These persons may be superintendents or their assistants. They may be college or state-department personnel. They may be curriculum coordinators or directors. They may also be classroom teachers who serve as resource teachers for a system, or supervisory personnel whose major role is supervision of classroom teachers.

Much time and energy have been put into research on the relationship between principal behavior and operating patterns. The evidence brought out by this research points to the fact that the principal is the key figure in the school and that his behavior does affect teachers' behavior, both positively and negatively. Many of these research studies have been under the auspices of the W. K. Kellogg Foundation, and from data based on Kellogg research projects in the public schools of Florida, Hines and Grobman concluded:

Not only are parents and pupils affected by the manner in which the principal carries out his duties but teachers feel and act differently as a result of this principal action pattern. Teacher satisfaction with human relations on the present job is higher in schools with relatively democratic principals than in schools with relatively autocratic principals. Teachers tend to use what experts consider good or desirable practices somewhat more often in schools with democratic principals than in schools with authoritarian principals. However, teacher-community relations, in terms of teacher feelings toward and interaction with the community, are not obviously affected. In the area of program change, the more democratic principals secure wider participation among those involved, and use a wider variety of procedures to produce change. (Since one criterion of democratic behavior is the extent to which others are involved in decision-making, this may be simply a matter

[3]*Ibid.*, pp. 215–216.

of definition of democratic behavior.) Teachers in elementary schools with democratic principals have significantly more favorable attitudes toward curriculum change than teachers in elementary schools with authoritarian principals. There is no significant difference between junior and senior high schools on this basis.[4]

One might reasonably infer from this report that secondary schools have changed their administrative methods of staff operation less than have elementary schools. The fact that the elementary schools place greater emphasis upon individual social growth and maturational patterns than do the secondary schools may help to explain this difference.

The wise administrator will on occasion lay aside the mantle of authority and mingle with his staff. When administrators shun their staff members socially, the gulf extends into the professional working relationship. If an administrator can mix comfortably in a social way with his staff, the authority that goes with his job can be better tolerated and staff members are usually more willing to produce for him.

Social activities are a necessary part of productive working groups. In a description of curriculum work in Hunterdon County, New Jersey, Woolf and Doll write:

> Activities of the articulation committees and study groups in Hunterdon County seem to thrive best where there is skilled leadership, a friendly atmosphere, and marked willingness to work. In the best-functioning groups, administrators treat teachers as their professional equals. Productivity is greatly enhanced by conducting meetings in comfortable surroundings and throughout the school day. Cooperative and friendly feelings are engendered to a point at which group members desire social contact with each other. This desire is indicated in part by members' interest in conducting dinner meetings for both social and professional purposes.[5]

[4]V. A. Hines and Hulda Grobman, "What a Principal Does, Matters," *Phi Delta Kappan*, XXXVII (April 1956), 309.

[5]Kenneth A. Woolf and Ronald C. Doll, "Curriculum Planning: A Regional Approach," *Educational Leadership*, 20 (December 1962), 169.

A summary of a research study by Banning concerned with attitude toward curriculum change among junior high-school teachers speaks of teacher-principal relationships:

To teachers who are favorable toward helping in a new program the relationship that seems to exist between teachers and administration is of prime importance. If teachers feel they have the encouragement of the school leaders, they look upon change with approval. They also do something about it, for they like having a part in policy making.... Interaction is the keynote. The teachers indicated in interview after interview this strong factor of interaction, the most valued relationship being that with the principal of the unit. Whenever teachers felt genuinely accepted by the principal, they felt more highly favorable toward the entire leadership. It is evident that in the school unit itself the feeling of friendliness with the principal makes the greatest difference in the whole picture.[6]

A study by Bidwell concerned with factors highly productive of teaching satisfaction and enthusiasm has a direct bearing on teacher-principal relationships. This study found that one of the most important factors that produced satisfaction was a feeling of professional status among the teachers. Several ways of encouraging this feeling of professional status were given in the study. It was suggested that teachers need a sense of freedom to plan their own work. They need to participate in formulating policies concerning salaries, working conditions, and the educational program, to share in setting salary schedules, and to participate in curriculum construction. An important, necessary second factor was found to be fair and sympathetic professional leadership. The influence of the principal was felt more keenly than that of any other person by the teachers who participated in Bidwell's study. The influence of the superintendent was felt less strongly; however, because of his responsibility for the selection and behavior of the principals, his leadership is of primary importance in teacher satisfaction.[7]

[6]Evelyn I. Banning, "Here's How Teachers See It—Teachers' Attitudes Toward Curriculum Change," *New England Schools Development Educational Council* (April 1956), p. 54.

[7]Charles E. Bidwell, "Administration and Teacher Satisfaction," *Phi Delta Kappan*, XXXVII (April 1956), 286.

Change takes time, and most teachers do not want to be pushed into doing their work differently. As a curriculum-building program progresses, administrators will have to learn to accept new ways of working with their staffs. Using a new technique or method becomes an established habit only after repeated practice and a feeling of success.

Since our interest lies in the role of administration in curriculum building and improvement, we need to know all we can about the effects of administrators upon the curriculum and the teachers who implement it in the classroom. Some of the studies that have been done relative to administrative behavior and its effects on teacher behavior shed a great deal of light on the perennially slow pace of curriculum change.

The State of New York has been extremely active in the investigation of ways of accelerating educational change. Under the leadership of James E. Allen, Jr., Commissioner of Education, three publications of especial note have been produced.[8] Two of the publications, by Brickell, were financially supported by the Fund for the Advancement of Education of the Ford Foundation through a grant to the New York State Education Department. Recognizing that New York City schools required separate treatment, the City completed early in 1961 a comprehensive survey of its own experimental programs. The results of this survey were published in the spring of 1961 under the title, *Portals to the Future.*[9]

Brickell's study of New York State offers some real insight into the effects of administrators on curriculum change. From the evidence in this study, one might reasonably conclude that classroom

[8]See all three publications for a well-planned and efficiently organized attack on the problem of encouraging and implementing educational change in the public schools of New York State and elsewhere.

Arthur D. Morse, *Schools of Tomorrow-Today* (New York: Doubleday and Company, Inc., 1960).

Henry M. Brickell, *Commissioner's 1961 Catalog of Educational Change* (Albany, New York: State Department of Education, 1961).

Henry M. Brickell, *Organizing New York State for Educational Change* (Albany, New York: State Department of Education, 1961).

[9]*Portals to the Future: Research, Experimentation and Evaluation* (New York: Board of Education, 1960). (Annual report of the Superintendent of Schools, 1959–1960.)

teachers have known for some time that little significant change in practice could occur in the schools without the support and interest of the administration.[10]

Brickell, who served as Consultant on Educational Experimentation to the Commissioner of Education in New York State, studied New York City schools and thirty additional public-school systems that were representative of all types of communities in the state. In the description of his sample, Brickell states:

Active, well-financed suburban school systems were chosen somewhat more often than other types because it seemed important to study closely those conditions which are most conducive to rapid educational change, according to previous research into community types. The fact that such school systems were generously represented gives a special urgency to the conclusions in this report. If the conditions which affect change even in well-supported, suburban schools are as described here, then in other school systems not so richly endowed with resources the pace of change is presumably even slower, the direction even less certain.[11]

He is aware of the roles played by the public, the board of education, the administrators, and the teachers in the dynamics of instructional innovation:

There are two distinct groups of people who might be expected to influence structural change in the local public schools: the public, which is external to the institution, and the profession, which is internal to it. The process of educational change is determined by the relationships of these two groups: the public and the board of education as external, the administrators and the teachers as internal.

Calls for distinctly different educational results tend to come from outside the school itself, that is, from the public and the board which represents that public.

When the school is asked to produce a different kind or a different quality of education, some rearrangement of its instructional elements may be in order. One of the tasks of a chief administrator

[10]Brickell, *Organizing New York State.*
[11]*Ibid.,* p. 13.

—such as a superintendent of schools—is to take external demands for different results and translate them when necessary into new patterns for organizing the elements of the institution (or for changing the elements).

Like the teachers, the administrator has a stake in maintaining stability so that traditional results can be produced. He also must be particularly responsive to demands for new kinds of results. Schools are usually structured so that the chief administrator can be kept responsive to external demands: The superintendent serves in a contract relationship to a lay board of education.

Even before new demands are expressed locally, an administrator who sees nearby schools like his own making structural changes may anticipate the local pressures which are to come and move in advance to meet them.[12]

In his study of New York schools Brickell expresses several concepts of vital importance to curriculum practices. First, as noted in Chapter I, there must be a valid recognition of the school as a social institution. The school, like any other social institution, tends to remain relatively stable and resists attempts at restructuring. This resistance on the part of the school is justified in terms of the concomitant drop in production that would occur if a change were made in its elements.[13] Research in the field of group dynamics supports the idea that productivity drops when changes are made in elements of an institution or manufacturing concern.[14]

In order that new content or methods of teaching may be incorporated into curriculums, one needs to anticipate a drop in production until staff members have been able to form new habit patterns. Curriculum-improvement programs have too often been based upon the false assumption that teachers could quickly assimilate directives regarding new ways of teaching. Frustration has often been the result of such an assumption: frustration for the administrators because teachers did not respond readily or enthusiastically, and

[12]*Ibid.*, pp. 19–20.
[13]*Ibid.*, p. 19.
[14]Lester Coch and John R. P. French, Jr., "Overcoming Resistance to Change," in *Group Dynamics: Research and Theory*, 2nd ed., ed. D. Cartwright and A. Zander (New York: Row, Peterson & Co., 1960), pp. 319–341.

frustration for the teachers because they had no part in establishing the new procedures and no time to compensate for the drop in production while they learned new ways.

New ways can be introduced by administrators, if they plan jointly with the teaching staff and if they are not overanxious for immediate results. Change takes time, from the point of view both of the teacher and of the students while they exchange old habit patterns for new ones.

SUPERINTENDENT'S ROLE
IN CURRICULUM BUILDING

The office of the superintendent of schools is, in most systems, the focal point of progress or stagnation for the entire school system. It is from this office and this instructional leader that the entire school system gets its educational tone. Look at any city, town, or rural school system of your acquaintance. Make an attempt to measure the progress that this school system is making currently. Ask yourself questions such as these:

1. Is the school system turning out the kind of graduate who is well prepared, by the standards of its community and today's world, to meet the challenges of living in our contemporary society?
2. Does the system give its school population a balanced education in terms of individual needs and societal needs?
3. What is the educational philosophy of this system, and does its philosophy show in its curriculum?
4. Are the school buildings appropriately designed and equipped, within the limits of local and state financial ability, to do the kind of educational task that should be done for the pupil population today?
5. What evidence can you find to show that this school system is making advantageous use of local communications media to inform its patrons of its problems and plans for the future?
6. If the school system is "on the growing edge" of contemporary practices, can you find evidences of uses of modern instructional aids? Are there multiple tests, tape recorders,

film strips, overhead projectors, in addition to files of available enrichment materials?

7. How have recent school-bond issues fared in this school system?

8. What has happened to teachers' salaries in the past ten years?

9. What special services are available, such as those provided by guidance counselors, school psychologists, doctors and dentists, librarians, speech therapists, and remedial reading teachers?

10. What is the pupil-teacher ratio in elementary and in secondary classrooms?

11. Is there a professional library or materials center in the system for the teaching personnel?

12. What is the percentage of teacher turnover in the system? Do good teachers tend to stay and grow professionally with the system, or do they move on as soon as a better salary opportunity presents itself?

A host of other questions could be asked as one tries to evaluate a school system in terms of the kind of educational assignment that has been given to it by its community. The above list of questions, however, will suffice to give some insight into any school system. The answers to them will begin to illustrate strengths and weaknesses of any public-school system.

The most logical place to go for answers to our questions is the office of the system superintendent. Here is the nerve center of any public-education system. From the superintendent's office, one may receive an over-all view of the operational pattern of a school system. This office is involved in decision making that affects all instructional, noninstructional, and pupil personnel within its jurisdictional limits.

As the instructional leader for a school system, the superintendent sits at the apex of the administrational ladder. Earlier in the book, it was pointed out that there is an hierarchy in public education just as there is in business or industry. From the point of view of curriculum building and revision, the superintendent is in the most advantageous position of all school personnel to exert constructive leadership. Just as the classroom teachers look to the building principal for leadership and direction, so the principals look to the superintendent. If the superintendent is aware of his power to encourage creative growth and curriculum change in his system, and if he has the knowledge, skills, and techniques necessary to do so, there are few limitations to curriculum building.

A creative superintendent is rather rare, just as creative principals and classroom teachers are atypical. For that matter, creative persons in all walks of life are relatively rare, since most of us are creatures of average potentials and abilities. What, then, is the role of the superintendent, realistically speaking, in an average school system with an average staff of principals and teachers? What can a superintendent do to encourage better curriculum-building practices, to increase staff resources, and to broaden perceptions of board members and citizens? Let us look at several possibilities for leadership within the realistic framework where a superintendent must work.

Perhaps the first step a superintendent can take is to return to a college or university campus and attempt to increase his professional knowledge. Numerous changes in administrative theory and practice have developed in the period from the close of World War II to the present. In 1959 Griffiths made this appraisal of the field of educational administration:

Much of what is now taught is composed of the testimonials of successful administrators, the folklore which has accumulated over time, and an odd assortment of promising practices. This material in interspersed with a few research findings, but these findings are largely restricted to the topics of school finance and organization. We are just beginning to introduce into the literature some of the findings of research in the behavioral sciences. The great job to be done is to develop a theory which can accommodate and illuminate the assortment of research from the behavioral sciences, the fact and fancy in our field, as well as point the way to new knowledge. This theory will enable us to sort our relevant facts, to give meaning to the batches of data we now have, and to disclose needed areas of study.[15]

[15]Daniel E. Griffiths, *Research in Educational Administration—An Appraisal and a Plan* (New York: Bureau of Publications, Teachers College, Columbia University, 1959), p. 5.

In the years which have passed since then, schools and colleges of education have greatly modified their programs. Many institutions of higher learning had, of course, begun this needed revision some time before Griffiths' report. Another giant step forward was the action taken in 1959 at the convention of the American Association of School Administrators.

It was at this convention that the school superintendents adopted a constitutional amendment requiring two years of approved graduate study at an approved institution as a qualification for membership in American Association of School Administrators, thus making this organization the first major national professional association in education to demand of its members specific qualifications.[16]

Some nine years earlier the W. K. Kellogg Foundation had set in motion a project known as the Cooperative Program in Educational Administration.[17] As a result of the Kellogg research studies, increased interest by professional organizations, and the many contributions of the behavioral sciences, the entire complexion of public-school administration has changed. Superintendents who wish to learn about the changed emphases and procedures will need to return to school, in addition to attending their professional conferences and keeping up with professional reading.

In addition to returning to graduate school for further study, there are several other ways for the superintendent to assist in curriculum building. As the top administrator in the school system, the superintendent can lend enormous support to curriculum projects in the schools. If the projects are to have a chance to succeed and make an impact upon the instructional program, they need the enthusiastic support of the administration. The superintendent can take the initiative in suggesting projects. He can convince his teachers that he endorses their ideas and attempts to improve the curriculum. He can offer tangible evidence of his full support by sitting in as a member

[16]*Toward Improved School Administration* (Battle Creek, Michigan: The W. K. Kellogg Foundation, 1961), p. 8.
[17]Hollis A. Moore, Jr., *Studies In School Administration* (Washington, D. C.: American Association of School Administrators, 1957).

of the central curriculum committee. In this role, he can work with the teachers and other administrators in the planning of contemplated changes. When the superintendent sits in on the original stages of the program, teachers will be inclined to feel that acceptable ideas stand a good chance of coming to fruition. This feeling on the part of the teachers always leads to higher morale and increased zeal. Another important role for the superintendent is that of creating time and opportunity for members of the curriculum committee to work together. From the superintendent should come the initiative to create free school time for teachers to work on curriculum.

As the educational leader of the entire school system, the superintendent should set an example for all his assistants by creating an atmosphere of freedom and experimentation in the schools. By his manner and his approach to teachers and principals, he can show them that he is open-minded and supportive of their experiments with new practices. He can encourage an experimental outlook on the part of all his instructional staff by lending his support to their efforts.

The superintendent can also help by making provisions for evaluation of all new curricular proposals and by encouraging the use of many different evaluative devices. It is often helpful if the superintendent points out to his staff that the most adequate measure of the success or failure of experimental programs is reflected in the behavior of the pupils. Some standardized testing materials will be used to gather data; however, if the emphasis is placed upon pupil behavior, data gathering will be directed toward indications of the development of desirable behavior changes. This kind of thinking represents, in itself, a healthy attitude on the part of the school system.

The superintendent of schools exerts a powerful influence upon the teachers, and the growth of the system rests in his hands. Teachers and principals are well aware of this power, and when it is directed toward support of their interests, they feel encouraged to experiment with curriculum. When the superintendent shows teachers he is vitally interested in and appreciative of their attempts to improve, there is a great potential for growth in professional competency.

SUGGESTED READINGS

Banning, Evelyn I. "Here's How Teachers See It—Teachers' Attitudes Toward Curriculum Change," *New England School Development Educational Council,* (April 1956), pp. 53–55.

Bidwell, Charles E. "Administration and Teacher Satisfaction," *Phi Delta Kappan,* XXXVII (April 1956), pp. 284–287.

Brickell, Henry M. *Organizing New York State for Educational Change.* Albany: State Department of Education, 1961.

Callahan, Raymond E. *Education and the Cult of Efficiency.* Chicago: The University of Chicago Press, 1962.

Cay, Donald F. "Selected Teachers' Expressed Judgments Concerning Barriers to Curriculum Improvement." Unpublished doctoral dissertation, University of Florida, 1960.

Griffiths, Daniel E. *Research in Educational Administration—An Appraisal and a Plan.* New York: Bureau of Publications, Teachers College, Columbia University, 1959.

Hines, V. A., and Grobman, Hulda. "What a Principal Does, Matters," *Phi Delta Kappan,* XXXVII (April 1956), pp. 307–309.

Krug, Edward A., *et al. Administering Curriculum Planning.* New York: Harper & Brothers, 1956.

Moore, Hollis A., Jr. *Studies in School Administration.* Washington: American Association of School Administrators, 1957.

Morse, Arthur D. *Schools of Tomorrow—Today.* New York: Doubleday and Company, Inc., 1960.

Mort, Paul R., and Cornell, F. G. *American Schools in Transition.* New York: Bureau of Publications, Teachers College, Columbia University, 1941.

Portals to the Future: Research, Experimentation and Evaluation. New York City: Board of Education, 1960.

Pritzkau, Philo T. *Dynamics of Curriculum Improvement.* Englewood Cliffs, N. J.: Prentice-Hall, Inc., 1959.

Toward Improved School Administration. Battle Creek: The W. K. Kellogg Foundation, 1961.

IV

THE TEACHER'S ROLE
IN CURRICULUM BUILDING

The teacher, now as always, is the focal point of any curriculum. From the teacher comes the spark that ignites the pupil's enthusiasm for learning. Like other persons, teachers possess varying degrees of skill: some have more innate aptitude than others, and some have had better preparation. Since all teachers have a great stake in the building of better curriculums, one way to improve curriculums would be to improve teachers' training in subject matter, in psychology, and in methods.

The success or failure of most teaching-learning situations has always been largely dependent upon the art and skill of the teacher. Who else in the school has the chance to touch so many pupils' lives so closely? As the professional person closest to the pupil, the teacher both nurtures and implements curriculum change. Although major changes in curriculum must have administrative support, many of the original ideas for changes come from the alert teacher.

What is it that the outstanding teacher gives to the pupils and to the classroom atmosphere that makes an exciting adventure out of learning? A teacher who inspires pupils to deepen their insights and to widen their intellectual horizons is one of the strongest aids to curriculum improvement ever known. In searching for an explanation of some teachers' success, we might look at a poetic expression of teaching strength. Kahlil Gibran, in a description of teaching, states it in this fashion:

No man can reveal to you aught but that
which already lies half asleep in the dawn-
ing of your knowledge.

The teacher who walks in the shadow of
the temple, among his followers, gives not
of his wisdom but rather of his faith and
his lovingness.
If he is indeed wise he does not bid you
enter the house of his wisdom, but rather
leads you to the threshold of your own
mind.[1]

One of the key concepts in Gibran's picture of teaching is faith in the learning potential of the individual. With faith in the ability of the individual pupil to help educate himself, the teacher becomes a resource person and a facilitator. He helps his pupils to open doors in their own minds.

All persons will not agree with this concept of teaching. Some will feel that the major role of the teacher is to put facts, figures, and knowledge into the student's mind. Many would believe that filling the minds of pupils with facts is the only way to make them follow the teacher. With this outmoded concept of good teaching, the pupil is never supposed to outdo the teacher but always be ready to follow. According to this concept, the teacher is always the leader and the pupil the follower, whereas the other concept permits the pupil as well as the teacher to assume leadership.

An outstanding teacher helps shape the future through daily assistance to pupils in the classroom. The pupils go out of the teacher's classroom into other classrooms, and then take their places in communities. As the outstanding teacher works with pupils, he senses his contribution to the ongoing process of education. A mental image created by the teacher in the classroom may serve as a spur to one or more of his students years later. The teacher knows that his daily work may have effects that reach far beyond the present.

UNDERSTANDINGS NEEDED BY TODAY'S TEACHERS

In order for a teacher to operate effectively in the classroom, he must first know all that is possible about the students with whom he

[1] Kahlil Gibran, *The Prophet* (New York: Alfred A. Knopf Co., 1953), pp. 56–57.

is to work. He should be familiar with their developmental levels, their emotional ties, and their cultural environments. A teacher cannot possibly reach his students if he cannot understand their yearnings and their desires, however temporary they may be.

Every sculptor cannot be a Michelangelo; yet, every good sculptor has a contribution to make. So it is with teaching. There are teachers who accomplish unbelievable goals with their students, while others who work equally hard fail to achieve any major successes. It is as difficult to define this teaching talent as it is to explain the special gift of Michelangelo. It is inherent in the person. Does this mean, then, that only the exceptionally talented teachers should stay in the profession? No, it does not; however, it does mean that each teacher must assess himself and his abilities in the light of his teaching success.

The teacher, like the leading actor in a play, has some set lines to enact—teaching the required material for the particular grade level. However, the method of presentation and scope of his teaching is mostly up to him. It is in the teaching that the teacher becomes a true artist or remains a transferer of knowledge. We have all known teachers who have magnetic personalities, ones who know instinctively how to reach into the minds and emotions of others. With personal magnetism and the mastery of their subject matter, such teachers have made remarkable contributions to the profession and the world. We have also known less dramatic teachers, with a reserved but sincere and knowledgeable approach to teaching, who have inspired many young people in their search for intellectual goals. However, inherent in most all teachers is the desire to contribute something worthwhile to their pupils.

Curriculum building usually begins in the classroom of a particular teacher, in the genesis of an idea by an individual and its experimental use in the classroom. This is one facet of curriculum building whose importance has not been sufficiently recognized by curriculum experts. Sometimes, although acknowledgement is made of the teacher's contribution, it is apparent that small value is placed on curriculum improvement that comes about through teachers' efforts within the classroom. Some experts stress administrative leadership as being vital to curriculum improvement, while still others have concentrated on the foundations of curriculum. The fact remains, however, that the teacher and his interrelationship with the student are at the heart of the whole process of curriculum building.

Two basic concerns of educators, relative to curriculum building, have been the needs of the society and the needs of the individual. These strong concerns have led to many modern curriculum practices. If we had not had such staunch supporters of the dual responsibility of the curriculum to the society and the child, how would we have been able to develop the core curriculum or the ungraded primary school? How could we have known that special guidance services were so important to high-school students as they tried to plan their future? Would it have been possible for community schools to become so popular and functional in an educational system that did not place a high priority on societal needs? Could we have developed programs of distributive education or cooperative training that allow high-school pupils to learn, work, and earn at the same time? Would it have been possible to utilize effectively both homogeneous and heterogeneous groupings of pupils? Many advances in curriculum practices have developed because of the mutual needs of the society and the individual.

SOME PROBLEMS OF THE PROFESSION

Because the teachers in today's schools are products of two different eras of teacher education, it is understandable that not all teachers see any given educational problem from the same perspective. In the decade of the forties, the traditional emphasis on the teacher as a supplier of knowledge and discipline began to lessen. Teachers who did their college work from then to the present were, and are, taught to see their major role as a guide or resource person. They feel obligated to help pupils help themselves, an approach quite opposite from the traditional one.

These two groups of teachers are so far apart in their thinking and practice that it is a major task to get them to agree on anything. Yet, the leaders in curriculum-building projects have to work amicably with teachers holding both points-of-view. This is a gigantic task, and often the dilemmas posed by such extremes in philosophy and practice are relieved by acceptance of the status quo.

Beginning teachers, who are vital and enthusiastic, become discouraged when they run into undesirable attitudes on the part of older members of the faculty. As in any other profession, the teaching profession depends upon the younger members for new ideas and a sense of excitement. Beginning teachers should feel free to offer their ideas and to introduce new techniques with no fear of being isolated or shunned by other faculty members. If the established teachers greet new faculty members with open-mindedness, the new teachers will feel free to discuss and try out new ideas with them.

Another problem of the teaching profession is that many young women enter teaching each year on a temporary basis. These young women have no serious intention of remaining in teaching. They have no intention of becoming career teachers. They only use teaching as a stopgap on the road to marriage or as a means of gaining a second income in the family. This makes for an exceedingly large turnover in teaching personnel, and the resultant lack of stability in faculties tends to weaken the school's curriculum. It also tends to weaken articulated educational experience for pupils. With a rather large group of new teachers falling into this category each year, and a group of married women back in teaching as a temporary source of a second income in the family, attempts at professionalization are almost certain to be less than satisfactory. Career teachers, like career lawyers, doctors, engineers, scientists, and business persons, are intrinsically motivated toward improvement of their profession. Temporary persons in any profession do not possess this same degree of motivation. What can be done to help such temporary classroom teachers understand their role in curriculum building?

A good beginning lies in the recognition by administrators that most teachers, both career and temporary, desire to have a part in planning the school's curriculum. They need freedom and opportunity to try new projects in their classrooms. Participation in classroom experimentation tends to keep the teaching-learning situation alive, vibrant, and absorbing for both teachers and pupils. Most teachers have some ideas of their own that they wish to implement in their classroom. Encouragement to try out these ideas could be the beginning of building a better curriculum.

HOW TO ENCOURAGE TEACHERS TO PARTICIPATE

In order for teachers to feel encouraged to participate in curriculum-building programs, they need to feel right about their relationships, both personal and professional, with the administration, with other teachers, and with pupils and parents. These four areas of relationships were studied by the author as the subject of his doctoral dissertation.[2] The central hypothesis of the study was: Certain factors that teachers see as barriers to curriculum improvement can be isolated.

From the study of selected secondary-school teachers came the following conclusions:

a. Strong indications were given by the teachers, in the data returned, that factors which they see as barriers to curriculum improvement can be isolated in the four areas of relationships investigated in this study.

b. If principals wish teachers to feel encouraged to participate in curriculum-improvement activities, they need to include teachers in planning and policy-making decisions which affect school operation.

c. If principals want teachers' support and loyalty in curriculum-improvement activities, they need to consult their teachers more often before making arbitrary decisions which affect daily school routine.

d. In order to feel encouraged to participate in curriculum-improvement activities, teachers need to feel that other faculty members are supportive of curriculum change.

e. Teachers need to feel that most other faculty members accept them, both professionally and socially, in order to feel encouraged about participation in curriculum activities.

[2]Cay, dissertation.

f. Interest by pupils in class planning and evaluation procedures will encourage teachers to participate in curriculum-improvement activities.

g. If teachers are to feel encouraged to participate in curriculum-improvement activities, they need to see changed behavior patterns in the pupils they teach.

h. In order to feel encouraged to participate in curriculum-improvement activities, teachers need to know that their goals and practices, in connection with the pupils, are similar to those of the parents.

i. In order for teachers to feel encouraged to participate in curriculum-improvement activities, parents need to let them know that they are interested in and supportive of the school program.[3]

SOME CHARACTERISTICS OF SUCCESSFUL TEACHING

What makes a successful teacher? Is it a specific facet of personality or knowledge or training? Is it possible to measure the qualities of successful teaching? Perhaps an imaginary walk down a corridor of a school will demonstrate one manifestation of quality teaching, or the lack of it.

Have you ever visited a school in the middle of a normal busy day and walked through its corridors? During your walk through the building, what signs were you able to detect that indicated a good teaching situation? Looking in an open classroom door gives all kinds of pictures to an experienced observer. Just looking carefully at pupils and their expressions is one of the most enlightening ways of searching for quality teaching. Their expressions may reflect interest and eagerness, or boredom and resentment because they are forced to spend time in the classroom. Facial expressions of pupils tell quite a story about the kind of teaching going on within a classroom.

One thing is certain: If the teacher is enthusiastic about his teaching, pupils tend to pick up his zeal. Enthusiasm in teaching is as contagious as measles among children. To generate enthusiasm, a teacher needs a deep, abiding faith in people. Add to this faith a love

[3]*Ibid.*, pp. 196–207.

of learning for its own sake and a special love for a specific subject-matter area. These ingredients will charge the classroom just as carbonated water charges a soft drink.

Although highly enthusiastic persons in any line of work are rare, a high degree of zeal is a distinguishing characteristic of successful teaching. Wiles speaks of quality teaching as:

> ... an unusual contribution by a unique personality, to pupil growth or to the development of the school program. He may not teach like anyone else. He has qualities and abilities different from anyone else. He has studied himself and the learning situation and has decided how he can be most useful; he is giving himself fully and successfully in the implementation of his decision.[4]

A successful teacher usually generates sparks of interest in his pupils. It may be a spark that will start a lifetime love of learning, or it may inspire a deep interest in the teacher's own area of specialization. Most teachers, when asked what encouraged them to choose teaching as a career, will name a former teacher as one of their strongest motivating agents. Somewhere in their educational experiences, most teachers found another teaching personality that touched their own deeply and permanently. Although many reasons can be found to explain the impression a particular teacher makes on the life of a student, there is a saying that is particularly apt: "What you are speaks so loudly that I cannot hear what you say." Expressed in the language of teachers, one might say: "Much more is caught than taught." Haan, in reference to teacher personality and the curriculum, states a similar idea in this simple, clear way: "What the teacher *is* educates children."[5]

The following list points out some additional ways of making classroom teaching more successful:

a. Varying methods of presentation and kinds of materials.
b. Maintaining better than average knowledge of a specific subject-matter area.

[4]Kimball Wiles, *Teaching for Better Schools* (Englewood Cliffs, N. J.: Prentice-Hall, Inc., 1959), p. vi.

[5]Aubrey Haan, *Elementary School Curriculum: Theory and Research* (Boston: Allyn and Bacon, Inc., 1961), p. 293.

c. Adequately understanding the student peer culture of one's classroom.
d. Including the learners in class planning and evaluation experiences.
e. Increasing the student's responsibility for his own learning.
f. Keeping communication lines short and clear.
g. Decorating the classroom in an attractive fashion, with student participation.
h. Studying the principles of human growth and development, and using this knowledge in teaching.

TEACHER APPROACHES TO BETTER CURRICULUM

What can an average teacher in an average community do to improve the curriculum in his school? In a hypothetical average community, some teachers are well trained, others are poorly trained, and some are between the extremes. Some buildings are old and dilapidated; others are new and modern. Some of the instructional materials are outmoded, and some are up-to-date. The community may be a large city with a terribly overcrowded school system; the community may be a little town; or it may be a farming area with a small, isolated school. All of these school systems are good, fair, or poor, depending mainly on the value system of the community they serve, which, in turn, determines the available tax base for funds and the quality of the teachers.

Regardless of the kind of school system, there are ways in which teachers may help to build better curriculums. Teachers are more influential than they realize. Parents, through the eyes of their children, look to teachers for leadership in new kinds of thinking and varied approaches to content. Experimental teaching, which means being willing and able to apply some new approaches to the teaching-learning situation, is also its own reward. Such teaching tries, and normally succeeds, to enrich the learning experiences for teachers and pupils. With enriched classroom learning and interested pupils who take home to their parents the results of experimental teaching, a classroom teacher lays the foundation for curriculum improvement within his classroom. Admittedly there are some risks involved in experimental teaching. There is always the risk that things will not work out as anticipated, and the new method may fail. Some parents will resist any change from traditional procedures; such is the nature of human beings. Yet progress has usually gone forward in spite of resistance. Classroom teachers need to be more daring in their daily teaching. They need to take the risks involved in experimental teaching for the sake of the rewards that can be gained in better curriculums.

An excellent way to begin curriculum improvement is to evaluate the existing curriculum in terms of today's needs. A teacher should measure his practices against those of other teachers and against research findings in the social sciences that bear on the professional task of teaching. This type of comparative measurement usually leads to curriculum change and improvement on the teacher's part.

In being cognizant of tendencies that teachers, as a professional group, seem to possess, one cannot overlook the avid desire to verbalize as demonstrated by most members of the profession. One needs to realize that excessive verbalization often slows down any real, constructive action. Teachers will often agree intellectually with new concepts, yet fail to put the concepts into action. If teachers are aware of this tendency, perhaps they will be more willing to act. There can be little real curriculum change without action in the classroom.

Although classroom teachers are important agents in curriculum change, as Brickell points out, the kinds of curriculum change that they make is limited to their own classroom unless they receive administrative support and interest.[6] However, much can be done within a classroom to build better curriculums, and there is no better place to start. New subject matter, a different method of presentation, a novel way of working with pupils, modern methods of evaluation, fresh usage of instructional materials—all these may lead to a better curriculum. Pupils are usually anxious to experiment, and if a teacher is willing to try something original and fresh, even on a limited basis, it will tend to enrich and stimulate their thinking.

[6]Brickell, *Organizing New York State*, pp. 22–26.

Here are some questions a teacher may ask himself as he begins to build a better curriculum:

a. Do I know enough about my pupils?
b. What kinds of additional information regarding my pupils might lead me to a clearer understanding of their learning processes?
c. Is the pupil's family life a factor in his progress, or lack of progress, in my classroom? If so, how does it affect him?
d. How do my pupils see me? Am I personally acceptable to them?
e. Am I truly stimulating pupils to reach for *new* growth and *new* knowledge?
f. Do I use enough variety in classroom procedures?
g. What are some fresh approaches to teaching my special area to pupils?
h. How could I use a novel approach to my next unit of work?
i. What kinds of new instructional materials do I need to learn how to use?
j. Am I in touch with new content material in my field? If not, how can I bring myself up to date?
k. Am I attending enough professional conferences, meetings, and institutes to be aware of what other school systems in my region are doing?
l. What was my most successful teaching experience of last year? What was my least successful one? Why?
m. Do my pupils give evidences of growth, mentally and emotionally, as a result of our having worked together?
n. Am I willing to risk criticism for the sake of trying something of an experimental nature with my pupils?
o. How does my principal feel about trying new approaches to teaching?
p. Have I talked over my ideas recently with my principal?
q. Will my experimental methods disturb other teachers?
r. How çan I encourage my pupils to help in planning our units of study this year?
s. What kinds of contacts do I have with my pupils' parents?
t. Are there some ways in which parents can help us enrich our classroom experiences?

u. Do some of the parents have special talents or skills that they might be willing to share with us?

v. What kinds of activities do I participate in outside of school? Do they help to satisfy my need for adult companionship, friendship, and recreation?

w. Am I paying enough attention to my own physical condition? Do I exercise regularly in order to keep in good condition and to release my emotional tensions?

x. Have I visited another school recently to see how other teachers attempt to do the same job I do in my own classroom?

y. Is my spiritual life as strong as it should be?

z. What can I do to help remove unnecessary duplications from my classroom teaching?

The foregoing list of questions gives some indication of the scope of curriculum improvement. *Curriculum is the entire school program and all the people involved in it.* The points of attack are countless; yet an attack on any one of these points will begin the process of building better curriculums. To plan an attack and implement it is the role of the classroom teacher. Such an attack requires a study of what one is currently doing, an evaluation of the results of this study, a plan for future improvement, and the action-implementation of the plan. In simple language, one has to plan his work and work his plan.

CURRICULUM IMPROVES
AS SELF-UNDERSTANDING INCREASES

Teachers may also begin to build better curriculums by learning more about themselves. The secret of successful living lies in self-knowledge and the recognition of our personal strengths and weaknesses, capitalizing on our strengths and trying to overcome our weaknesses. This quest for self-knowledge is indicative of a growing, expanding personality. Teachers, in order to build better curriculums, need to enlarge their own horizons.

The whole field of perceptual psychology is gaining wider acceptance as an aid to understanding human behavior. In a discussion of teachers' perception of self and the teaching role, Combs and Snygg point out:

How a teacher behaves in the classroom depends not only on how he sees his students and the situation in which he is involved, but also, upon how the teacher sees himself. Like everyone else, teachers are seeking personal adequacy and their behavior will be deeply affected by the degree of adequacy they have achieved. Students are responsive to teachers' personalities and there is much evidence to show that well-adjusted teachers produce better-adjusted students while poorly-adjusted teachers have negative effects upon those they teach.
... In a very large measure, effective teaching is a process of sharing self with others. Inadequate personalities find this very difficult to do. The ability to involve and share self with others is highly dependent upon the individual's own feelings of his personal adequacy.[7]

Teachers, like other people, are all seeking personal adequacy. Perhaps we can derive from this search for personal adequacy a series of behavioral guidelines that will enrich our teaching and improve our curriculums. Let's look at our own classroom behavior.

What kinds of behavior do we exhibit in our classrooms? On some days do we succeed better than on other days? How do our experiences outside of school influence what we do in the classroom? Do family problems exert pressures on our teaching duties? Is it possible to "leave our worries on the doorstep" and concentrate our entire thought and energy on our teaching?

As teachers, if we are honest with ourselves, we must admit that we exhibit many different kinds of classroom behavior. Like other people we are happy, sad, moody, concerned, witty, humorous, serious, lighthearted, or gay, depending upon the occasion. Like other people, teachers have inherited and acquired personality characteristics. Our behavior is primarily caused, as Combs explains, by what seems to us to be so:

[7]Arthur W. Combs and Donald Snygg, *Individual Behavior: A Perceptual Approach to Behavior* (New York: Harper & Brothers, 1959), p. 406.

People do not behave according to the facts as others see them; they behave in terms of what seems to them to be so.[8]

This concept should help explain why different pupils react differently to the same phenomena. This concept should also help us to understand and honor individual differences in behavior among the teachers with whom we work, as well as individual differences among pupils. A great deal has been written concerning individual differences among pupils, but little attention has been devoted to individual differences among teachers who work on the same faculty or within the same school system. Individual differences are certainly as common and as valid among teachers as they are among pupils. To give us greater insight into how we may work more efficiently with teachers in building better curriculums, more research is needed in assessing their individual differences.

Because we are human, our dispositions will not always be serene. As a matter of fact, there are days when pupils' behavior would make "a sinner out of a saint." Let's take the case of the elementary-school teacher on a gloomy, rainy day with 25-35 ten- or eleven-year-old pupils who want and need exercise. If the school does not have gymnasium facilities (and countless elementary schools do not) the rain keeps the teacher and her wiggly pupils confined to the classroom. As most elementary teachers know, such a situation turns a usually calm, patient teacher into an edgy, anxious person. No one is really at fault. The pupils are reacting as young children normally do to inclement weather, and the teacher reacts in adult fashion to her inability to provide the necessary release from tensions that the playground period usually gives the pupils.

Similar special days occur on the secondary-school level, too. Take the occasion of the high-school teacher trying to impart knowledge to a group of enthusiastic adolescents on the Friday of the homecoming game. The normal value system of adolescents places football at the top of the scale, far above English, French, mathematics, history, or biology. Although teachers often enjoy football too,

[8]Arthur W. Combs, "Seeing Is Behaving," *Educational Leadership*, XVI (October 1958), 21.

their enjoyment is on an adult level, which is vastly different from the adolescent level. On such a day as this, high-school youngsters are almost in a state of panic. In the life of the secondary-school teacher, such a day may be accurately compared to "sitting on a powder keg with a short fuse." These special days tend to turn secondary-school teachers into vigilantes, who anticipate trouble rather than avoid it. The examples given are not uncommon in elementary and secondary schools. On such days, teachers are wise to swim with the pupil tide rather than against it.

What about problems in family life outside of school? Suppose some member of your family is ill and you have spent the better part of the night caring for him. Your patience is apt to be rather short in the classroom the next day. Your preparation is also bound to be thin, and questions from pupils for which you are unprepared may keep you in a defensive position all day. Your normal classroom behavior is colored by your personal problems of any consequence, and it is almost impossible to leave your worries at home. Most of us take our anxieties with us to our work. Teaching, because of the many demands made upon teachers by pupils, does tend to lessen one's conscious concern with his problems; yet the personal cares remain until they are resolved. Teachers' classroom behavior can be made more stable if they recognize that family problems do impinge upon professional behavior. At such times teaching procedures should be modified to meet the teacher's psychological and physiological needs. Pupils are usually more adaptable than teachers. At times like those described, teachers need to protect themselves. Such occasions justify placing teachers' welfare above pupils' welfare.

If children were able to behave as adults, they could be more understanding of teachers' problems, but they are not; nor should we expect them to be. Children live primarily on the level of immediacy. Teachers, for the most part, live on a level of long-range planning. Pupils like a great deal of activity. Teachers prefer intellectual pursuits. This difference of interests tends to put teachers and pupils at cross purposes, unless teachers honor in their curriculums this basic activity need of pupils. Writers and researchers in psychology and education have repeatedly emphasized the activity needs of children. Curriculums such as the Life Adjustment Curriculum, Developmental Needs Curriculum, and the Core Curriculum have incorporated this activity need with the social, emotional, and intellectual needs of youth.

A guiding principle that will help teachers to build better curriculums is that *both the pupils and the curriculum are in a constant state of development and change.* The evolutionary nature both of the individual and of society has been extensively documented by cultural anthropologists and sociologists. If teachers can learn to accept change as normal and desirable, they will find themselves on the road to building better curriculums. The pupils in today's classrooms, at almost all levels of education, have grown up with change as an accepted phenomenon. Most pupils welcome it. Change means variety to them, and a different way of doing something usually interests them. Teachers may also learn to welcome change and use it for their own teaching enrichment. To be able to live comfortably and constructively with change means one less hurdle for the teacher to cross.

TEACHER-PUPIL RELATIONSHIPS

One of the major goals of teachers is to effect changed patterns of behavior in their pupils. Bush states it in the following manner:

...the teacher occupies a leadership role in relationship to the student, inasmuch as he arranges the situation so as to engender changes in the student's behavior.[9]

Teachers must remember that they are in the most favorable position to engender behavioral change. If this change takes effort—and most changes do—the pupil is unlikely to make the effort without stimulation from the teacher. Pupils will make little effort if no one asks them; like the rest of us, they are inclined to do things in the easiest and least energy-consuming fashion if they can get away with it. If the teacher does not exert the necessary stimulus, he cannot

[9]Robert Nelson Bush, *The Teacher-Pupil Relationship* (Englewood Cliffs, N.J.: Prentice-Hall, Inc., 1954), p. 67.

expect much desirable change to come from the pupils. *Undesirable* behavioral change will probably occur, but nothing particularly constructive will be forthcoming without teacher initiative.

Another major goal of teachers is to encourage and promote learning. Bush describes this basic function of teachers:

All relations in the school—those of teacher-pupil, counselor-teacher, teacher-stenographer, teacher-custodian—are to promote pupil learning. The professional relationship is considered effective, regardless of personal feeling, as long as it accomplishes the purpose for which it has been established.[10]

Whether or not the teacher is able to effect behavioral change in pupils, he can usually promote some measure of learning. To a greater or lesser degree, some kind of learning takes place in the classroom. As long as some learning occurs, the teacher has fulfilled a primary function.

What is the relationship between teachers' liking for their pupils and pupil performance? In Bush's study of relationships between teachers and pupils, he found that *mutual liking* of teacher and pupil appeared in only 15 per cent of all the cases studied. One might conclude that a teacher's liking for students appears to be unrelated to teaching competence. On the other hand, in Bush's study the findings suggest that pupils' liking for their teacher is directly related to an increase in ability to learn:

... the findings of this study suggest that the personal liking of a pupil for his teacher is one of the most powerful factors in bringing about an effective learning relationship between the teacher and the pupil. It seems reasonable therefore to suggest that a strategic task for the teacher is the cultivation on his part of the personal liking of his pupils for him. This requires a teacher who is skilled, sensitive, and adjusted in the area of personal relationships and who is able to handle his relations with pupils objectively rather than as a source of meeting his own personal inadequacies. Learning is enhanced markedly when teachers make themselves personally acceptable to pupils.[11]

[10]*Ibid.*, p. 19.
[11]*Ibid.*, pp. 187–188.

If pupils learn better when their teachers are personally acceptable to them, it would appear that some thought about making themselves more acceptable to pupils is in order for teachers. This does not mean that teachers should make a career out of getting pupils to like them. It does, however, indicate that teachers could well afford to cultivate behavior and to employ teaching methods that appeal to their pupils. When one listens to pupils' descriptions of their teachers, it is apparent that they usually have the greatest respect and liking for those teachers who are "hard but fair." What this means is that a teacher may expect performance so long as he is acting fairly in the eyes of the pupil. To be fair to pupils means to accept students as they are and to assist them to grow intellectually, socially, and emotionally. Being fair imposes an obligation upon teachers to help pupils to try to understand their own difficulties and to give them opportunities to work their own way out of problem situations. It means giving pupils the freedom to make mistakes and also letting pupils know that teachers make mistakes too. It means communicating to pupils that the classroom is a cooperative learning experience. It means being willing to admit that *teachers do not know the answers to all questions.* Establishing a relationship with pupils by using these techniques means that the atmosphere of the classroom will be "freed for learning and growth." In a classroom with such an atmosphere, teachers give clues to pupils as they work together. These teachers do not give pupils all the answers to all their questions, but, instead, they share their knowledge so that pupils have to do some reasoning, thinking, and reaching on their own. Teachers in such classrooms help pupils to seek the *why* of the situations they explore together, and teachers and pupils move together into the realm of inquiry.

Thelen speaks of what seems to him to be the greatest educational need for today's youth as he describes personal inquiry:

Personal inquiry is driven by strong needs of individuals, and the educational requirement is to place the learner in a carefully chosen environment in which he can discover the insights he needs to behave more intelligently![12]

Teachers can help pupils to achieve the needed insights at all levels

[12]Thelen, *Education*, p. 14.

of schooling, with each insight being appropriate to their developmental levels. Teachers should create a classroom environment that encourages learners to seek and reach for the understandings they need. A joint sense of learning and partnership—where teachers and pupils learn together—can assist pupils and teachers in this exciting quest for understanding. Mutual interest and sharing of the goal of deeper insights will enrich the curriculum of any classroom.

SUGGESTED READINGS

Brickell, Henry M. *Organizing New York State for Educational Change.* Albany: State Department of Education, 1961.

Bush, Robert Nelson. *The Teacher-Pupil Relationship.* Englewood Cliffs, N. J.: Prentice-Hall, Inc., 1954.

Cay, Donald F. "Selected Teachers' Expressed Judgments Concerning Barriers to Curriculum Improvement." Unpublished doctoral dissertation, University of Florida, 1960.

Combs, Arthur W., and Snygg, Donald. *Individual Behavior: A Perceptual Approach to Behavior.* New York: Harper & Brothers, 1959.

Haan, Aubrey. *Elementary School Curriculum: Theory and Research.* Boston: Allyn and Bacon, Inc., 1961.

Jersild, Arthur. *When Teachers Face Themselves.* New York: Bureau of Publications, Teachers College, Columbia University, 1955.

Leese, Joseph, *et al. The Teacher in Curriculum Making.* New York: Harper & Brothers, 1961.

Murphy, Gardner. *Human Potentiality.* New York: Basic Books, 1958.

———. *Personality—A Biosocial Approach to Origins and Structures.* New York: Harper & Brothers, 1947.

Sharp, George. *Curriculum Development as Re-education of the Teacher.* New York: Bureau of Publications, Teachers College, Columbia University, 1951.

Spears, Harold. *The Teacher and Curriculum Planning.* Englewood Cliffs, N. J.: Prentice-Hall, Inc., 1951.

Thelen, Herbert A. *Education and the Human Quest.* New York: Harper & Brothers, 1960.

Wiles, Kimball. *Teaching for Better Schools.* Englewood Cliffs, N. J.: Prentice-Hall, Inc., 1959.

———. *The Changing Curriculum of the American High School.* Englewood Cliffs, N. J.: Prentice-Hall, Inc., 1963.

V

THE ROLES OF PARENTS AND PUPILS IN CURRICULUM BUILDING

Two groups who should be encouraged to participate in curriculum building are parents and pupils. Let us think first about parents. Not only do they pay a large portion of the tax bill to support public schools, but they are intimately involved with the products produced by the schools—their children. Pupils are the raw material that parents send to school for teachers and administrators to refine and educate.

Although the ambitions of parents for their children differ greatly, most parents want the public schools to give their children the best possible education. For some parents this means preparation for college, while other parents want their children to be ready for additional vocational training. For still others, it means preparation to become self-supporting immediately upon graduation. Despite their varying ambitions for their children, almost all parents have some interest in what the school teaches their children and how it accomplishes this task. When citizens pay taxes for public education, they have a vested interest in public schools. Parents are entitled to assist professional educators in major curriculum-building ventures, and if they are not given this opportunity, the educators are inviting criticism.

There are those in public education who feel that parents have no business being involved in curriculum building. This position does not seem to be justified, although experience in some communities where the planning and preparation for parent participation was not adequate may explain why some educators feel this way. Parents need to be involved in any major curriculum-improvement program that is worth the time and effort spent on it.

The question does not seem to be whether or not to involve parents in major curriculum-improvement programs. It does appear to be *when* to involve parents, *how* to involve them, and *which* parents to invite as representatives of the community. Some schools are located in a community where the educational level of parents is high; other schools are situated in areas where the educational level is consistently low. A third group of schools—and this is the largest group—is located in an area where both extremes occur, along with all the gradations from one extreme to the other. Parents who are representative of the community will bring a realistic viewpoint to curriculum building and will tend to keep educators' feet on the ground.

Naturally enough, the parents who participate will be most interested in their own children. Teachers should be aware of this and recognize the need to encourage interest in all the children. By working slowly with parents and expressing interest in their children first, teachers may help them become aware of their child's needs in relation to those of the other children in the school. Teachers are in a good position to point out similarities between the parents' own child and other children. Most parents are able to make the shift in attitude from "my child" to "our children," and with assistance from teachers the shift can come early in the working relationship. Once the parents and other participants begin to see the total picture of curriculum as affecting all the children in the school, the program is underway. Helping parents to enlarge their perspectives beyond their own child to other children is a task particularly suited to the teachers and one that they do very well.

The need for close communication between teachers and parents has been much discussed in educational literature, and professional education courses place a definite emphasis upon this area of relationships. The elementary school and junior high school are generally more deeply involved in close parent-teacher relationships than is the secondary school. Actually, students may need a closer relationship between parents and teachers at the high-school level than they do at the earlier levels.

REPORT OF PARENT-TEACHER RELATIONSHIPS

As part of a study of the working relationships in which secondary teachers are involved, the author investigated parent-teacher relationships, particularly their possible effect upon teachers' participation in curriculum-improvement activities. A brief report on the results of that study may be helpful to the reader at this point.

The sample, in the research study, consisted of one hundred secondary classroom teachers who taught in grades eight through twelve. The communities represented included rural areas, small urban areas, and a large metropolitan suburban area. The teachers in the sample participated in the study on a voluntary basis, with each group of teachers being given a sixty-item questionnaire at one time, and a follow-up interview that double-checked original responses. The teachers in the sample were asked to rate each of the sixty items on the questionnaire on a 0-4 point scale, in terms of how each item would affect their feelings about participation in curriculum-improvement activities, either on an individual or school-wide basis. The rating scale used was:

4 Would *encourage* my participation in curriculum-improvement activities.

3 Would have *no effect* on my participation in curriculum-improvement activities.

2 Would *limit* my participation in curriculum-improvement activities.

1 Would *prevent* my participation in curriculum-improvement activities.

0 I am *undecided* as to the effect it would have on my participation in curriculum-improvement activities.

The results of the study were organized under the following two sub-hypotheses:

(a) *When teachers feel that their goals and practices are very different from those of the parents of their pupils, this will appear to them as a barrier to curriculum improvement.*

(b) *If teachers feel that parents are nonsupportive of the school
program and lack interest in it, this situation will be interpreted by them as a barrier to curriculum improvement.*

Under (a) above, the following interpretation of data appears:

The teachers in the sample indicated by low ratings given to
items in the area of teacher-parent relationships that, when they
felt there were great differences between their goals and practices
and those of the parents, there were many barriers to curriculum-
improvement apparent. Barriers to curriculum-improvement were
identified by 23 to 54 per cent of the teachers, arising from this
difference in goals and practices between teachers and parents.
Teachers were particularly blocked by parents who did not up-
hold high standards of work from the pupils.

Under hypothesis (b) above, the following interpretation of data
appears:

Teachers in the sample indicated by low ratings given to items in
the teacher-parent area of relationships that, when parents were
not interested in and supportive of the school program, many
barriers to curriculum improvement arose. The teachers indicated
that they felt the need of parental support and interest very
keenly. More "limiting" or "preventive" ratings were given to
items in the area of teacher-parent relationships than in any other
area under investigation in this study. Barriers were identified by
38 to 63 per cent of the sample, arising from lack of interest in
and nonsupport of the school program by parents.

The area of teacher-parent relationships stood out by a wide
margin, in the judgments of the teachers in the sample, as the area
in which items were rated most frequently as causing barriers to
participation in curriculum-improvement activities. The evidence
obtained from Questionnaire ratings and the answers to Interview
questions served to confirm their judgment that relationships between teachers and parents had a far greater effect upon their
feelings about participation in curriculum-improvement activities
than any other area under investigation.[1]

It is interesting to note that of the four areas of relationship under

[1]Cay, dissertation.

consideration—those of teacher-administrator, teacher-teacher, teacher-pupil, and teacher-parent—the study revealed that the area of teacher-parent relationships caused the greatest number of potential barriers from the teachers' point-of-view. The study also revealed that other equally important barriers to participation in curriculum-improvement activities exist in the school, such as lack of time, inadequate financial resources, and lack of instructional materials. Because the study was confined to secondary teachers, it should be recognized that there may be different barriers for elementary teachers. More research is needed.

IMPORTANCE OF PARENT-TEACHER COOPERATION

Why is it so important that teachers and parents know each other and learn to work together? Certainly a primary reason involves the welfare and educational growth of the individual child. When a pupil comes to school, he brings many of the ideals, attitudes, and prejudices of the home with him. What his parents feel to be important is likely to be of vital significance to the child. It is difficult for the pupil to pursue one value system at home and another at school; yet this is often the case. One of the best ways to bring different value systems into harmony is for people to work together on problems of mutual concern. Programs that seek to build better curriculums seem ideally suited as a way for improving parent-teacher relationships.

Parents already work in many ways to help the public schools. They work in the Parent-Teacher Association, as room mothers, and on boards of education. They participate in local Citizens Committees, and, on the national level, may work with the National Citizens Committee for Better Schools. Some school systems use parents and other lay citizens to serve as advisory members of curriculum councils. This type of citizen participation is well defined and concisely outlined in the 1961 Yearbook of the Association for Supervision and Curriculum Development.[2] In this publication, the *advisory nature*

[2]Association for Supervision and Curriculum Development, *Balance in the Curriculum* (Washington: National Education Association, 1961), pp. 187–191.

of citizen participation in curriculum-improvement projects is carefully delineated. Although the major responsibility for building better curriculums rests with the professional educators, advice and assistance should come from parents and other qualified lay citizens, since our public schools do belong to the people who pay taxes for their support and control them through boards of education.

Parents and other lay citizens often criticize the public schools, sometimes with justification. Many times, however, the criticism is caused by inadequate information and misunderstanding of the facts. When one looks at the persons involved and the unjust criticisms that are often founded on emotion rather than fact, one may conclude that many of these critics are representative of a minority segment of any community. Sometimes, however, criticism of the public schools has been a goad to re-evaluation of content and practices. It has served as a stimulus to educators to become more aggressive in defending their practices or to revise their practices in terms of current needs. Out of turmoil, an improved social order often arises. Out of the criticisms of public education in the past fifteen years, a better school and a vastly improved curriculum may arise. Today we see certain advantages, which have grown out of criticisms, currently operative in our schools. The greatly enriched and improved curriculums in science and mathematics, both at the elementary and secondary levels, are among the more conspicuous examples. Other fields of study have also been substantially enriched both in their content and methods; namely foreign languages, physical education, English, reading, and social studies.

There is no doubt that parents have constructive roles to play in assisting educators to build better curriculums, but educators must help parents become oriented. Educators must remember that almost every parent regards his child as someone very special. This is as it should be, but this common parental attitude may cause misunderstandings with educators. The educator sees the pupil as an individual, but because of his relationship with the pupil in groups, he may see him only as one of many pupils. Parents, on the other hand, tend to look at their child as a separate entity. Educators tend to forget that parents are motivated by sentiment where their own child is concerned. It is relatively easy to be objective about some one else's child, but it is almost impossible to feel that same objectivity about your own child.

From research studies in industry, Roethlisberger offers some keen insight that should be helpful to educators in their dealings with parents:

> The human being is a social animal and a social animal is not merely—in fact is very seldom—motivated by matters pertaining strictly to fact or logic. However, to conclude from this statement that therefore all human responses not strictly logical are illogical or irrational is a false distinction. Most human behavior is neither logical nor irrational; it is nonlogical; that is to say it is motivated by sentiment. To eliminate such nonlogical conduct would be to destroy all values and significances, everything which for most of us makes life worth living.[3]

If educators understand that parents' behavior, where their children are concerned, is caused mainly by sentiment, much frustration may be removed.

Whenever one speaks with teachers regarding relations with parents, the most common complaint is, "The ones I need to see never show up." Who are these missing parents? What is their background, home life, social standing in the community, and economic status? What prevents their attendance at school functions?

Parents in this category present teachers with an almost insurmountable problem. They are often referred to as "in absentia" parents. The children of such parents may be the ones with whom the teacher is having the greatest amount of difficulty. Why don't these parents, who need to confer with the teacher, come to the school? White reports findings of a research study which gives some insight into the reasons for non-attendance of some parents:

> Many of the parents whom we really need to know are the ones who find it impossible to attend school functions or do not feel comfortable in the social situation because of feeling of social

---

[3]F. J. Roethlisberger, *Management and Morale* (Cambridge: Harvard University Press, 1952), p. 31.

inadequacy or the belief that they cannot associate with those parents who have better clothes, better education, and more material things. Parents who cannot bring themselves to attend these group functions must be sought out, and a special effort must be made to know them in a situation which is comfortable for them. If we are to realize the ideal that the public schools belong to all the people, we must use every possible technique to bring into the school community these parents who are threatened by social situations.[4]

Most schools have parents like those described. If, as educators, we could understand that some of these parents criticize us and our work as a *defensive* measure to help them buoy up their own personality structure, not in a vicious manner but rather as an attempt to prove that they, too, should be heard, then we could try to give them the status they need in the parent groups. In this way we could better our relationships with this group of parents, who could then contribute within their ability to the school.

NEED TO MODERNIZE CONCEPTION OF THE SCHOOL

As educators work with parents, two of the most dangerous areas of possible misunderstanding are those of new methods and new content. Contemporary teachers, especially the younger teachers, are apt to forget that the modern school is a far different type of school than the one attended by most of the pupils' parents. Like other citizens, parents tend to be critical of new methods and content that they do not understand. Bossing has indicated that ". . . it is a general tendency for adults to idealize the education they experienced."[5] If parents do idealize the education of their youth (and it seems that we all tend to idealize many youthful experiences) then a major portion of the educator's role is to help parents understand modern education through careful, accurate interpretation. Johnson

[4]Verna White, *Studying the Individual Pupil* (New York: Harper & Brothers, 1958), pp. 120–121.
[5]Nelson L. Bossing, *Principles of Secondary Education* (Englewood Cliffs, N. J.: Prentice-Hall., 1955), p. 8.

and Michael suggest the importance of this task to educators, and ways in which it may be accomplished:

The average layman carries in his memory a picture of education as he experienced it. All people did not have satisfying and successful experience with school; many of them dropped out before completion of all minimum requirements. Unless the layman is provided with the experiences to reconstruct his perception of the school and its activities, he will use this memory picture as a standard of evaluation. Thus, when his children bring home reports that deviate from his expectations, he has much the same reaction as when his wife brings home an unfamiliar brand of coffee. The new brand may be good, but being unfamiliar, it immediately arouses suspicion. When new practices in school come to his attention without his having had an opportunity to understand them, he is likely to react with disfavor.

Providing opportunities for discussion of information about new or different ways of teaching or new content is an important means available to teachers for helping the layman to modify and improve his conception of school work. Through much discussion and improvement of the layman's understanding of what the schools attempt to do, the standards by which he will inevitably evaluate the results are brought into harmony with the goals toward which the school is working. The importance of this step is further realized when it is considered that the parents and laymen are going to evaluate the school whether their evaluations are sought or not.[6]

Parents should receive assistance from educators. It is well worth the effort, for as parents achieve understanding, they tend to become both cooperative and supportive. McCloskey, in a discussion of the rights and responsibilities of citizens regarding the schools, addresses the following warning to educators:

We can refrain from careless statements or ineptly phrased debate which infers that we question a citizen's right to approve educational policy. Such intemperance undermines public con-

[6]Earl A. Johnson and R. Eldon Michael, *Principles of Teaching* (Boston: Allyn and Bacon, Inc., 1958), p. 67.

fidence in our professional competence and strengthens the arguments of those who would preempt our professional functions. We cannot reject a citizen's right to participate in the educational affairs of their children. We can, and should, exercise the leadership which will make public participation more enlightened and effective.[7]

Unfortunately, there are many educators who need such a warning. Schools depend, for their very existence, upon the goodwill and understanding of the citizens of the communities served by them.

WORKSHOPS AS AN AID TO UNDERSTANDING

It would help parents and other laymen if educators staffed a community workshop prior to any major attempt to coordinate parent-educator efforts in curriculum building. At a workshop, parents would ask questions such as those in the following list, and the ensuing discussion would bring about some common understandings regarding modern educational philosophy, purposes, and practices.

1. Why is it important for our school to revise its curriculum?
2. What will we gain for pupils by use of new content and methods?
3. Will the teaching load be lessened or increased through the use of the new plan?
4. Do we consider the curriculum as the academic program or the entire experience of the school?
5. What is the basic educational philosophy of the teachers and the school?
6. How can parents understand the "educator's language"?
7. Are we helping or hindering our children when we assist them with assigned homework?
8. Will the proposed new curriculum serve all the pupils or will it favor a select segment?
9. Why is so much emphasis placed upon individual adjustment of the children in today's schools?

[7]Gordon McCloskey, "Who's Responsible for What?" *Phi Delta Kappan*, XLIII (December 1961), 137.

10. Why are the mathematics and science programs getting more emphasis than English, foreign language, and social sciences?
11. How can parents be of the greatest help to the teachers?
12. What is the most important area of curriculum improvement needed as we start the program? Why?
13. How much time will this program involve for the parents who take part and work with teachers?
14. Will parents' ideas about curriculum improvement be given equal opportunity for discussion along with those of the educators?
15. How much will such a curriculum program cost us?
16. Is the ultimate goal worth the expenditure of time, effort, and money?

The timing of a community workshop is important. Four or five meetings should be sufficient to create enthusiasm and generate some understanding and interest. The leadership of such a workshop, sensing that the groups are ready for action, should then move into the curriculum-building program while interest is high.

As discussed earlier, parents need some modernization of their concepts of educational purposes. They also need to understand what educators are talking about when they use professional language. Parents need a chance to be heard and to be informed pleasantly, informally, and in a professional manner. By providing such an opportunity through the creation of a workshop, educators may remove much potential frustration from their attempts to gain community support for curriculum change. The unpleasant feeling that parents want "to run the schools" does not seem to exist in communities where the public has been informed before major changes are made. Many forces in a community may bring pressure to bear upon the schools. Through enlightened school leadership, most of these pressures can be of a supportive nature rather than an antagonistic one. Educators have little to fear from parents provided they learn to work cooperatively with them.

Another vital function served by a community workshop is giving opportunity to parents and educators to become acquainted. They need to know each other informally, on a social level, before they try to work together on curriculum building. Like any other groups of persons, parents and teachers have some common elements in their thinking and also many diverse elements. Research and experience document the fact that persons who know each other work together better. In the first session or two of a community workshop, time and opportunity should be created for participants to talk informally and to begin to know each other. It is very difficult to try to discuss educational philosophy and practice with a stranger; yet educators have often expected such discussion without a necessary warm-up period.

Brickell's findings, in his study of New York State schools, illustrate the potential strength of parents and citizen groups.

> Parents and citizens groups in most communities do not exert a direct influence on the adoption of new types of instructional programs, but their influence is decisive when exerted.[8]

In a community workshop, when a major curriculum change is contemplated by local educators, the potential inhibitory factors contained in the parent groups can usually be removed. Most major curriculum-improvement projects stand a far greater chance of success with citizen support than without it. In fact, it is almost impossible to achieve a change of major significance with active opposition from citizen groups.

Any curriculum-building project of major scope should include representative parents and interested citizens as members of an advisory council, but minor curricular innovations may be handled best by school personnel. For example, a change in scheduling, provided that it did not alter arrival and departure time from school, would not call for parent participation. On the other hand, a basic change in the teaching of reading would call for parent preparation and participation.

PUPILS' ROLE IN CURRICULUM BUILDING

Pupils, like parents, should have some voice in curriculum-building projects. Once again, as with parents, the question is *when* to include

[8]Brickell, *Organizing New York State*, p. 20.

pupils, *how* to include them, and *which pupils to include.* As the major consumer of the public schools' products, the pupil, according to his maturity and experience, should have some voice in what he learns and how he learns it.

With good leadership from teachers, pupils will go to most any extreme to try to make a new type of learning succeed. The inherent vitality of youth is favorable toward curriculum change and improvement. Because pupils become bored with too much sameness and yearn for something different, a teacher need not hesitate to try something new. Instead of rebelling against change, the normal course of action for the pupils is to welcome it. What greater gift could a class bring to a teacher who wishes to experiment?

In working with pupils in a new program, teachers must realize that they need to see some evidence of progress. Curriculum building needs to have both short-range and long-range goals. With pupils, the short-range goals seem to have most meaning since they have a sense of immediacy about their living and studying. Pupil interest may be strong in the beginning, but without a sense of accomplishment it can wane rapidly.

Achievement test scores, intelligence test scores, aptitude test scores, and sociological and psychological test scores may all be utilized in building better curriculums. For example, as a result of studying test scores, many writers, both in the liberal arts disciplines and in professional education, have noted the tendency among American educators to underestimate the learning capacities and abilities of our youth. A sizable portion of our youth can do much more learning at an earlier stage than we are presently asking them to do. Test scores give one indication of unused potential and may offer clues to building better curriculums that will give pupils the opportunity to fulfill their inherent potential.

Another way in which pupils' abilities may be utilized in curriculum-building ventures is through pupil-interest surveys. Pupils' liking for a specific type of learning activity or a certain branch of subject matter does show a positive correlation with their success in this work. At least a part of a school's curriculum may be built upon pupils' expressed preferences. On the other hand, many areas of study may not be enjoyed by the pupils; yet, according to our concepts of the necessary educational ingredients for successful democratic living, some knowledge of them is essential.

If teachers are to plan classroom experiences that will hold pupils' interest, they need to include some learning that has application to daily living. Learning that is too far removed from daily life soon loses its sparkle for pupils. Students need to be able to see how their classroom work applies to daily living. For example, in the social studies class, an explanation of methods used to convince voters of the need for local referendums can be related to a local school-bond issue. Pupils want some material that seems realistic to them and from which they can draw significance for daily living.

As pupils mature and become more discriminating in their judgments, they too may be invited to participate in curriculum-advisory councils. The pupils' viewpoints are valuable in curriculum building, for they tend to be candid and relatively uninhibited. New ideas may be realistically pretested with the help of selected pupils. In addition, research studies in group dynamics have amply documented the fact that persons have a greater interest in the success of a program that they helped to plan. If they have the opportunity to be a part of the planning groups, pupils are more likely to work for the success of better curriculums.

In attempting to build better curriculums, teachers and administrators would do well to recognize the finding of Bush's study regarding differences of interests between teachers and their pupils:

> The interests of teachers as a group are directly opposed to the interests of pupils as a group. The teachers prefer verbal activities and related subjects, whereas the pupils select manipulative ones.[9]

If this difference is accepted and understood by curriculum planners, then a realistic use of pupil participation is apparent. Pupils can select, better than anyone else, the types of manipulative skills they would like to include in an improved curriculum.

Most pupils prefer learning that involves active pursuits and will rebel if too much stress is placed upon abstract learning. Work can

[9]Bush, *Relationship*, p. 192.

be included in most all classes that allows some activity of a physical nature for the pupil. Projects and displays made by pupils to illustrate certain aspects of learning give opportunities to pupils to do something with their hands as well as their minds. An excess of abstract verbalization frustrates pupils, and teachers need to beware of this type of teaching.

Although manipulative skills are used in art, music, industrial arts, typing, shorthand, home economics, physical education, agriculture, and science, some manipulative skills may also be incorporated in the traditional academic subjects. Many public schools are doing this, and have done it for a considerable period of time, but many more need to reorganize their academic subjects to include physical activity.

Because pupils have limits to the amount of time and energy they can profitably spend in academic pursuits, educators need to balance the academic side of the program with co-curricular activities. After a period of academic concentration, co-curricular activities act as a release valve and give pupils a chance to refresh themselves. Maintaining a proper balance between the academic and the co-curricular is a demanding task for educators and one that most of them do quite well.

An integral portion of any curriculum-improvement attempt is involved in creating better relationships between teachers and pupils. The establishment of rapport between teachers and pupils is paramount to curriculum improvement.

SUGGESTED READINGS

Association for Supervision and Curriculum Development. *Balance in the Curriculum.* Washington: The Association, 1961.

Bush, Robert Nelson. *The Teacher-Pupil Relationship.* Englewood Cliffs, N. J.: Prentice-Hall, Inc., 1954.

Cay, Donald F. "Selected Teachers' Expressed Judgments Concerning Barriers to Curriculum Improvement." Unpublished doctoral dissertation, University of Florida, 1960.

Cunningham, Ruth, and Associates. *Understanding Group Behavior of Boys and Girls.* New York: Bureau of Publications, Teachers College, Columbia University, 1951.

Kelley, Earl C., and Rasey, Marie I. *Education and the Nature of Man.* New York: Harper & Brothers, 1952.

McCloskey, Gordon. "Who's Responsible for What?" *Phi Delta Kappan,* XLIII (December 1961), pp. 137–140.

McKune, E. J. "Do Educators Want Laymen's Help?" *School Executive,* 75 (February, 1956), pp. 62–65.

Ojemann, Ralph H. *Personality Adjustment of Individual Children.* Washington: National Education Association, 1954.

Storen, Helen F. *Laymen Help Plan the Curriculum.* Washington: Association for Supervision and Curriculum Development, 1946.

———. "Role of Laymen in Curriculum Planning," *Educational Leadership,* 9 (February 1952), pp. 275–278.

White, Verna. *Studying the Individual Pupil.* New York: Harper & Brothers, 1958.

VI

EXTRINSIC FORCES BEARING UPON CURRICULUM BUILDING

Many forces, outside of the public school, have a direct or indirect bearing upon curriculum building. Because the school is a part of a community, the curriculum is, in a large measure, a reflection of the value system subscribed to by the community. The curriculum is also affected by state, business, industrial, national, and international values and policies. Some of the major extrinsic forces that help to shape curriculum will be discussed in this chapter.

HIGHER EDUCATION

Higher education, as the parent of the public school and the sole producer of its teachers and administrators, has the most direct effect upon curriculum building of all forces extrinsic to the public school itself. Because the people who teach and administer the public schools all come under the direct influence of the colleges and universities, the impact of college and university professors upon pre-service and in-service teachers is tremendous. As was pointed out earlier, teachers tend to teach as they have been taught.

Beginning teachers who possess a bachelor's degree have received their formal education in either a liberal arts college, a teachers' college, or a university. Regardless of which type of institution provides the bachelor's degree (and there are 1,200 institutions that enable their students to qualify for a standard teaching certificate[1]), each

[1]Research Division, National Education Association, *Teacher Supply and Demand in Public Schools, 1962* (Washington: N.E.A., 1962), p. 15.

teacher with a bachelor's degree has been given reasonably heavy grounding in traditional liberal arts subjects in the four-year period —exactly how heavy determined by the basic purpose and philosophy of the particular institution. Normally, the emphasis is heavier in the liberal arts college than in the teachers' college; yet it exists in both. In the university, the liberal arts subjects receive emphasis in the first two years of the general education program for all prospective teachers; this emphasis continues through all four years for prospective secondary-school teachers who have their major or their minor in a liberal arts subject.

Although the emphasis on liberal arts has not been so great for elementary teachers as for secondary teachers, the latest trend appears to be toward heavier emphasis. Such a trend, if judiciously encouraged, should give the prospective elementary teacher a more adequate background in one or two academic areas of knowledge. It should reduce the extreme breadth of elementary programs and lend a measure of concentration to them.

Many hours have been spent discussing whether teachers should have more subject matter and less professional education, or vice versa. Some liberal arts-oriented college professors have supported all subject matter and no professional education, while professional educators are inclined to support less subject matter and more education courses. There has been some progress made toward bringing these two opposing groups of professors together to consider future programs of teacher education. The major national force behind joint planning sessions for improved teacher education programs is the National Commission on Teacher Education and Professional Standards, commonly known as NCTEPS and sponsored by the National Education Association. Three national conferences, sponsored by such scholarly societies as the American Association for the Advancement of Science, the American Council of Learned Societies, the National Academy of Sciences, and NCTEPS have been held to consider this problem. These three conferences were convened at Bowling Green (1958), Kansas (1959), and San Diego (1960).[2] One of the principal outcomes of all three conferences was

²See G. K. Hodenfield and T. M. Stinnett, *The Education of Teachers* (Englewood Cliffs, N. J.: Prentice-Hall, Inc., 1961).

the agreement that teacher education should be an all-college or an all-university responsibility, with all departments involved in the preparation of teachers working together. The work of all departments or divisions within individual colleges or universities is usually coordinated by a Teacher Education Council. The membership of this council normally consists of staff members from the liberal arts division and the education division. This kind of institutional cooperation is certainly a step toward joint improvement of standards for the preparation of teachers. Regional and state TEPS groups are continually at work on the task of improving professional standards for teachers.

In reality, many subject matter-oriented educators and many education course-oriented educators are working toward the same goal. Both groups desire the most adequately prepared classroom teacher possible. In the next ten to twenty years, as we attempt to modernize the content courses and methods courses of pre-service and in-service teachers, one may expect increased cooperation between liberal arts professors and professional educators.

Some outstanding examples of curriculum studies in subject matter areas are given in the following list.[3]

Science
a. The Physical Science Study Committee (PSSC)
b. The Biological Sciences Curriculum Study (BSCS)
c. The Chemical Bond Approach Project (CBA)
d. The Chemical Education Materials Study (CHEM Study)
e. Science Curriculum Improvement Study
f. University of California Elementary School Science Project
g. University of Illinois Elementary School Science Project

Mathematics
a. University of Illinois Committee on School Mathematics (UICSM)
b. The School Mathematics Study Group (SMSG)
c. Ball State Teachers College Experimental Program

[3]Detailed information regarding sponsors of these projects and sources from which complete data may be obtained are given in the N.E.A. publication *Current Curriculum Studies in Academic Subjects* by Dorothy M. Fraser (Washington: N.E.A., 1962).

d. University of Maryland Mathematics Project (UMMaP)
e. Boston College Mathematics Institute
f. Developmental Project in Secondary Mathematics, Southern Illinois University, Carbondale
g. Studies at Stanford University: Geometry for Primary Grades Project; Sets and Numbers Project; Mathematical Logic for the School Project
h. Greater Cleveland Mathematics Program
i. Syracuse-Webster Elementary Mathematics Project, Webster College

English Language Arts

a. Commission on English of the College Entrance Examination Board
b. Position Paper of the National Association of Secondary School Principals (NASSP)
c. Report of the National Council of Teachers of English

Modern Foreign Languages

a. "FL Program Policy," Statement of the Modern Language Association
b. Position Paper of the National Association of Secondary School Principals (NASSP)
c. The FLES Program (Foreign Languages in the Elementary School)
d. Programs Developed under the National Defense Education Act
e. The MLA Testing Program

Social Studies

a. Joint Project of the National Council for the Social Studies and the American Council of Learned Societies (NCSS-ACLS Project)
b. Position Paper of the National Association of Secondary School Principals (NASSP)
c. Program for Improving the Teaching of World Affairs (ITWA)
d. Economic Literacy Series of the Council for the Advancement of Secondary Education (CASE)
e. National Task Force of Economic Education
f. High School Geography Project (HSGP)

Recent emphases in curriculum revision have been upon the academic subject matter areas. The foregoing list of curriculum studies in academic subjects is the result of a National Education Association Project on Instruction.

Most of these studies reported have been devised, at least in part, by college and university personnel in conjunction with professional organizations of public-school teachers and administrators. This listing of curriculum studies points out the potentially great impact of college staff members upon public-school curriculum building in the academic disciplines.

UNDERGRADUATE EDUCATION OF PUBLIC-SCHOOL TEACHERS

Liberal Arts Colleges

The greatest single producer of public-school teachers is the liberal arts college. Universities and teachers' colleges also produce a large number of teachers, but only in conjunction with their liberal arts college or division or department. Public-school teachers, according to traditional curriculum concepts, need a thorough foundation in one or more academic disciplines. State departments of education license or certify secondary-school teachers on the basis of required hours completed in a major and/or minor undergraduate program of study. Elementary-school teachers are also required to take subject-matter courses, although not in as great amounts as secondary teachers. In addition, prospective teachers are required to complete varying numbers of course hours in professional education, which usually includes the practical experience of student teaching during the junior or senior year.

Many liberal arts colleges prepare elementary-school teachers through a special department of elementary education. In recent years, increasingly larger numbers of the liberal arts colleges have added such departments so that they could compete for students with state universities and teachers' colleges. Traditionally, however, most liberal arts colleges have been concerned with the preparation of secondary-school teachers. Most liberal arts colleges contain a department or division of education that is primarily responsible for professional education courses and prepares students to meet state certification requirements.

Teachers' Colleges

Another institution of higher education that prepares a large number of public-school teachers is the state teachers' college. Many of the institutions so classified have recently been given university status. Because they are financed mainly with public funds, the teachers' colleges are generally less expensive than the liberal arts colleges. This financial saving is one attraction teachers' colleges have for students; another is their long tradition of a high degree of specialization in the professional training of teachers.

Today's state teachers' colleges began as Normal Schools with course work of two-year's duration. The era of the predominance of the Normal School as a teacher trainer existed principally during the late nineteenth and early twentieth centuries. In the evolution of these teacher-training institutions, they became teachers' colleges during the early 1900's. Later, during the 1940's and 1950's, they became state colleges or universities. Private teachers' colleges also train teachers and have been doing so successfully since before the turn of this century.

Universities

Universities, both public and private, contribute greatly to the education of public-school teachers. As the natural outgrowth of the college grown large, the university contains several professional schools or colleges within its administrative structure. As far as the education of public-school teachers is concerned, the university offers the academic disciplines through its college of arts and sciences. Pre-service teachers normally spend the greater portion of the first two years of their four-year programs in liberal arts courses that are designed to give all teachers a general background. The last two years are normally devoted to specialization, with part of the student's time in the college of his special area of training and the other portion in the college of education. The college of education gives the prospective teacher his professional course work, including student teaching, and prepares him for state certification. The arts and science college of the prospective teacher's specialization gives him advanced subject-matter course work and often offers subject-matter methods courses as well. For example, such courses as the teaching of science, the teaching of high-school English, or the teaching of elementary arithmetic are often taught in the college of arts and science.

Accreditation of Teacher-Training Institutions

Accreditation has long been a watchword in public education. Colleges producing new teachers are normally regionally accredited, and, in addition, many of them are nationally accredited. The national agency that is currently doing the major portion of evaluation and accrediting is the National Council for Accreditation of Teacher Education, commonly known as N-Cate.[4]

Such regional and national accrediting tends to bring some measure of uniformity to the preparation of public-school teachers. These accrediting agencies do not bring, nor do they desire to bring, conformity to a set of rigid standards. Rather, they seek to raise standards for the training of well-qualified persons to teach in the classrooms of America. N-Cate accreditation also assists in the free movement of qualified teachers from one state to another with no loss of credit hours earned. Within the teaching profession, such free movement is called "reciprocity of certification" and has been badly needed by qualified teachers who are part of our mobile society and who do move from one state to another.

The influences that regional and national accrediting agencies bring to bear on colleges producing teachers have an impact on public-school curriculum building. Well-qualified teachers cannot help working toward better curriculums for the pupils they teach.

The foregoing summary of the effects of higher education on curriculum building was confined to the first level of training, the

[4]N.E.A., *Teacher Supply and Demand in Public Schools, 1962* (Washington: N.E.A., 1962).

bachelor's degree. The discussion could be extended into the graduate level of preparation to include masters' degrees, certificates of advanced study, education specialist degrees and doctors' degrees. However, for the purpose of illustration of the undergraduate education of teachers, and its effects on curriculum building, this phase of their training should suffice.

COMMUNITY, STATE, AND NATIONAL INFLUENCES

The public schools and their curriculums are affected by the local community, the state, and the nation. Because our public education operates on a local-control basis, local community value systems exert the strongest effect on the curriculum. Next in importance comes the influence exerted by the state in which the public school system is located, and, finally, there is the influence of the federal government.

Community Values and Their Effects

Values vary from community to community, although certain types of communities with similar socio-economic and historic backgrounds have many common elements in their value systems. In all schools, community value systems have a strong influence on the curriculums.

Rural communities tend to value qualities such as hard work, a deep sense of religious duty, honesty, and a sense of pride in private ownership of property. These values, which are not all peculiar to the rural community, make themselves felt in the curriculum of the rural school as the teachers attempt to implement and reinforce the parents' value system.

Most rural secondary schools place a heavy emphasis upon the study of agriculture and agriculture-related occupations. They also tend to stress home economics for the girls. Many rural schools serve as centers for adult education and activities. For example, community canneries are often operated in the school by the agriculture and home economics departments. Some rural communities utilize the combined efforts of service clubs and industrial arts students to construct local recreational facilities such as baseball diamonds, tennis courts, shuffle-board courts, and swimming pools.

Urban communities, on the other hand, have value systems that tend to differ somewhat from those of their rural neighbors. Most urban communities contain a higher degree of sophistication than do most rural communities. Urban value systems usually encourage appreciation of art and music and heavy use of library facilities. Urban value systems are likely to approve activities such as dancing, bridge playing, foreign language study, and visits to museums. One example of the effect of the value system on the curriculum may be seen in the foreign-language program, for most urban schools have heavy language programs, often beginning in the early elementary grades and continuing throughout high school. Heavy emphasis upon business education, science, and mathematics also characterizes the urban high school, again reflecting the value which the community places upon these fields.

Many urban communities also have separate secondary schools for pupils who wish to enter the business or industrial world immediately upon graduation from high school. These secondary schools, formerly called trade schools, are known as vocational high schools.

Both rural and urban schools tend to emphasize in their curriculums the community values that are appropriate to their peculiar needs and locales. What actually results from these community values is a great variety in curriculums. The school consolidation movement throughout the nation has given a great boost to more adequate curricular offerings. Whether the school system concerned is rural or urban, community values make themselves felt in curriculum building.

States and Their Effects

The various states of the union also have their effects on curriculum building. From state to state these effects vary, because some state legislatures feel more strongly than others about certain courses becoming part of public-school curriculums. As was pointed out in an earlier chapter, state departments of education carry out the legal responsibilities of public education. Their function is to implement, through local school boards, the basic minimum requirements for public schooling within the state boundaries. In practice, much of the actual curriculum building is delegated to local school districts, with everything above the minimum originating with local school boards and local administrators. Hence, the American public school retains a large measure of local autonomy.

The National Government and Its Effects

Throughout the historical pattern of growth and development of America from its beginning to the present day, the federal government has been an advocate for and supporter of public education. Long-accepted examples of federal involvement exist in the support of land-grant colleges and of public-school programs in agriculture and home economics. More recent examples of the effects of federal government upon curriculum building are apparent in the science, mathematics, guidance, and foreign-language programs of our secondary schools, all of which have prospered and improved with the aid given them by the federal government under the National Defense Education Act of 1958. In addition to the aid given to secondary schools in the four areas mentioned, financial aid to college students in the form of loans has enabled many of them to complete an education which might otherwise have been impossible.

Solomon[5] indicates other important facets of federal aid to education: Civilian Conservation Corps, National Youth Administration, Federal Emergency Relief Administration, Public Works Administration, Vocational Rehabilitation Acts for veterans of World War I, II, and the Korean War, financial assistance to federally-impacted areas, federal loans for construction of college dormitories and other buildings, disposal of surplus property, appointment of students to the service academies, fellowships and traineeships.

There is no doubt that the federal government has a deep interest in public education. Part of this interest is a vested interest, since an avowed aim of public education has been the education of an enlight-

---

[5]Jack Solomon, Jr., *Federal Aid To Education* (Lincolnwood, Illinois: National Textbook Corporation, 1961), pp. 25–26.

ened citizenry for the express purpose of perpetuating our democratic form of government. The real issue, at the present time, is concerned with federal aid to public education, traditionally a state and local matter. Although some citizens fear federal support since the past shows that with support comes control, indications seem to point to increased federal support. Many nations operate their schools as an agency of the national government and under its direct control. Such a plan of school operation is distinctly less than desirable to most Americans, and they do not hesitate to raise their voices in protest at such a prospect. It would seem that, on the basis of the patterns of current federal aid to certain specific segments of public education, a new position may be achieved where federal aid and local control can be compatible.

Federal governmental expenditures have had a profound effect upon teacher-training, equipment, classrooms, and other aspects of curriculum building. As was mentioned earlier, the National Defense Education Act (1958) has greatly improved the curriculum areas of science, mathematics, guidance (counseling and testing), and foreign languages. At the present time, the United States Office of Education is supporting research projects with a million dollars to improve the teaching of English, and on April 11, 1965, President Lyndon B. Johnson signed the Elementary and Secondary Education Act of 1965, providing $1.3 billion for education, most of it designated for students in schools serving low-income families.

Current discussion of a national curriculum commission indicates a deep concern for some measure of uniformity of educational opportunity for all children, regardless of location. Paul R. Hanna, in an article published in 1961, under the title of "A National Curriculum Commission for Curriculum Research and Development," suggested the following goal:

Our desire to perpetuate and advance our cherished national values and institutions requires the creation of a nongovernmental, nationwide commission for curriculum research and development.[6]

[6]Paul R. Hanna, "A National Curriculum Commission for Curriculum Research and Development," *Phi Delta Kappan*, XLII (June 1961), 331–338.

Such a national curriculum commission might offer a partial cure for the increasing diversity of preparation of high school graduates. Although a commission would tend to bring a measure of *uniformity*, it is not even remotely suggested that it bring *conformity*. Much of the strength of American public education lies in the diversity that is the result of local value systems.

BUSINESS AND ITS EFFECTS ON CURRICULUM

Since the late nineteenth century, when industrialization moved into major prominence in America, the effects of business and industrial values and methods of operation have been keenly felt in the schools. Public-school administrators have, for the most part, attempted to operate their schools on the same philosophy as business executives. A businesslike set of operational methods and financing have been rigorously applied to public schools since the year 1900, according to a study by Raymond Callahan.[7] This study also discusses the effects of business and industrial methods upon public-school administration. When the administrators became convinced that business methods were the best methods to apply to public-school operation, our schools began to resemble factories. However, as Callahan points out in his preface, it is important to remember, "Education is not a business. The school is not a factory."[8]

Curriculum was, and is, deeply affected by the business-oriented outlook of public-school administrators. As the very heart of any educational program, curriculum demands close attention and continuous revision. Because many administrators have been devoting more attention to business management than to their curriculums, it is little wonder that curriculum is in the condition in which we find it today.

Curriculum is both quantitatively and qualitatively affected by the educational philosophy and practice of public-school administrators. Business practices, although sound in business situations, have

[7]Raymond E. Callahan, *Education and the Cult of Efficiency* (Chicago: The University of Chicago Press, 1962), p. 6.

[8]*Ibid.*, Preface, p. 1.

only a minor relationship to quality educational experiences for pupils in public schools. The kind of curriculum that is urgently needed in today's public schools will cost more money than any preceding generation has had to pay. (It should cost more, in the light of world conditions, economic conditions, social conditions, and the rapid expansion of both scientific and technical knowledge.) The future of America and any other nation rests surely and positively upon its youth. Deny the youth the best available curriculums and the richest possible school experiences, and you deny the future greatness of the youth and the nation.

In the past fifteen to twenty years, some business and industrial concerns have done much to aid colleges and universities, both philosophically and financially. The emerging pattern would seem to be one of cooperative ventures by business and education to share in the production of a better-educated and better-trained college graduate.

SOCIAL AND ECONOMIC FORCES AND THEIR EFFECTS

Each child is a part of many sociological groups: the family, the community, his peer group, the church, and the school. The child is a product of the society in which he lives; he is the living reflection of its economic structure, customs, mores, laws, religions, and intellectual achievements. Those who build curriculums must explore these societal factors in their respective locations before they attempt to design an educational program to meet the needs of the children.

The socio-economic conditions of different regions have a strong effect on the curriculum of the public schools and the kind of instructional program they offer. For example, school children in a coal mining town of West Virginia or Pennsylvania have curricular needs that are somewhat dissimilar to those of children who attend schools in the suburbs of large metropolitan cities. However, most public schools have pupils from all walks of life, each carrying within himself his own particular segment of society. It is in dealing with these varying backgrounds that our schools reach an almost idealistic height, serving as a great equalizer of class distinction based upon social and economic levels.

A first-grade classroom in a medium-sized Southern city gives a picture of the diversity of social backgrounds in one small group of pupils. Within a radius of ten miles of the school, these children came from environments that were as different as is possible in our American culture. The pampered daughter of the banker, the nuclear physicist's son, the custodian's son, the fireman's daughter, and the farmer's son represent a few of the differing backgrounds of the pupils. There was one pupil, however, who presented the greatest problem the curriculum builder faced. He, his parents, and eight brothers and sisters lived in a one-room hut with no water facilities of any kind. The environment from which the child came was squalid, to say the least, and he bore the odor of his environment, a constant source of unpleasantness to all the others in the classroom. The curriculum builder in this particular situation, as is so often the case, was the teacher. Her starting point was a bar of soap. Fortunately, the school was equipped with a bathtub, and after she encouraged the pupil to make use of this facility, much of the resentment and cruelty shown him by the other pupils slowly disappeared. With understanding, sensitivity, and an awareness of the tolerance inherent in children, the teacher turned the classroom into a cohesive, healthy, learning group.

As group members, children are subject to a multitude of influences. Performance in school, attitudes, behavior, and social growth are all affected by the standards of the groups to which the child belongs—standards that often vary from group to group. Although most adults have learned to adapt fluctuating values, it is difficult for children to know which set of values to choose. One set may represent "the easy life," while another set may look straight-laced and rigid. One of the tasks of the school, and of other community educative agencies, should be to develop a consistent set of values. Why shouldn't parents, religious leaders, educators, and other civic leaders work together and develop a set of values that children can live with at home, in the community, and at school? As we move forward with better curriculum building, more community agencies will become involved in helping educators to plan school experiences.

Currently, America and the rest of the world are in a state of transition from major concern with national sovereignty to concern with international cooperation. Curriculum builders will have to emphasize international awareness as one of the bases for future programs designed to serve American youth. Helping young people to understand other cultures that are different from their own and to rid themselves of prejudices based on emotions rather than on fact may well be two major objectives of curriculums in the coming years.

Desegregation—A Major Problem for Schools

In May 1954, the Supreme Court ruled that segregated public schools were unconstitutional. Since that time, most public schools have attempted to work out methods of complying with that historic ruling. Even one step toward desegregation of public schools in some communities meant a change of time-honored traditions and a completely new way of life. In some instances, the break with tradition was so great that every possible method of circumvention of the law was tried. In other communities, such a move meant that for the first time citizens were forced to reconsider their basic beliefs and values about other men and their children. Americans had to face the fact that although they had intellectually accepted the equality of educational opportunity for *all* children, this concept had not been made operative. It has always been easy to talk about equality for all children, but much more difficult to practice it and support it when one's own child is involved. Of all social changes affecting the schools, none takes precedence over desegregation.

Unfortunately, the public schools have been used as a scapegoat for many failures of a moral, political, and social nature. It seems to be easy for the American people to strike at the schools and ease their national conscience. Of considerable future importance, and closely related to desegregation, is the federal government's war-on-poverty program. It is extremely difficult, irrespective of color or race, to educate a person whose stomach needs nourishment and whose family needs adequate housing and clothing.

Many curriculum issues have been raised by desegregation in the schools. Some of these issues are directly connected with desegregation; others have been smoldering beneath the instructional lid for many years. The fact of desegregation has been a Pandora's box for public education, although, as in the myth, hope remains.

Critics of the public school have often condemned them for catering to the needs and interests of middle-class children and for slanting their programs in favor of college-bound pupils. Students of American secondary education have asked what the high school is doing for the pupil who goes directly into the labor market, either before or after graduation. As schools deal with desegregation problems, they are forced to revise their instructional programs to meet the needs of youth who may never go on to college. Considerable work has been done in some school systems to activate programs for culturally disadvantaged youth. The Higher Horizons Program of New York City and the Great Cities Project of the Ford Foundation are two prominent examples of such programs. In attempting to meet the educational, social, cultural, and psychological needs of disadvantaged youth, curriculums are planned with considerable realism in terms of everyday living. For example, some secondary schools have a daily schedule that makes possible part-time instruction and part-time employment. Making employment available is often the only way some pupils can be kept in school until graduation.

Desegregation has also raised the issue of whether or not the school should be involved in teaching human relations. As many others have been, this issue seems to have been resolved by necessity. As schools desegregate, a primary need for human-relations education is apparent, on the adult level as well as the pupil level. Human relations programs, upon which future programs can be based, have been conducted in Maryland, in Philadelphia, and in Cambridge, Massachusetts, to name three. Publications aimed toward better understanding of minority groups are available from the American Council on Education, the National Association for the Advancement of Colored People, the United Nations, and the National Conference of Christians and Jews. A source book containing teaching units that are very practical and useful is Gertrude Noar's book entitled *Teaching and Learning the Democratic Way*.[9]

Children moving from a segregated school to a desegregated school often have problems in academic achievement, but after these pupils have made up deficiencies in basic skills such as reading, writing, speaking, science, and mathematics, their levels of achievement rise rapidly. Segregated schools, by nature and nurture, are fundamentally unequal. Desegregated schools need to plan their curriculums with special staff members, space, and time available to enable the pupils who lack cultural background for academic success to catch up with more fortunate classmates.

Schools must plan for faculty desegregation as well as for pupil desegregation. Negro teachers are now in competition with white teachers, a relatively new position for them to hold. Recognizing this new position, Negro teacher-training institutions have enriched their programs. However, most Negro teachers are reticent to move into close working relationships with white teachers, and in most instances the white faculty members will have to take the initiative. Only when they begin to feel comfortable and secure, will Negro teachers be able to offer constructive leadership and assistance in building quality curriculums. One of the most important contributions of Negro teachers who join staffs in desegregated schools lies in their ability to help solve the problems of integration.

As a result of desegregation, desirable curriculum changes are bound to occur at the elementary and secondary-school levels of public education. Insights gained by teachers, administrators, and parents working together to assist pupils as they move toward integrated schools cannot help improving social and economic factors in our society that have so long been restrictive and prohibitive to many segments of our citizens.

[9]Gertrude Noar, *Teaching and Learning the Democratic Way* (Englewood Cliffs, N. J.: Prentice-Hall, Inc., 1963).

CULTURAL CHANGES AFFECT CURRICULUM

In our culture, the scientific and technological strides of the past century have greatly outdistanced the social and humanitarian advances. In order that a culture may be reasonably well balanced, it is imperative not to lose sight of the value of the arts, philosophy, and the social sciences. The arts tend to personalize learning and to encourage creativity within the individual, whereas science, by its method and nature, tends to objectify experience and findings, as does our industrial technology. In planning programs for gifted students, the arts should be emphasized as much as science and mathematics.

Although science and technology have made work lighter and living easier, there are many persons who find little meaning in their daily jobs and little satisfaction in daily living. With the tremendous progress in science and industry has come a lessening of the individual's feeling of worth and belonging, and many people have lost any sense of meaning or purpose as they go about their jobs of earning money and raising a family. Efforts should be made in curriculum building to enhance the individual's self-concept and to teach him ways to identify with others in his community, state, nation, and world.

Our population is highly mobile. No longer do people spend their entire lives at one address in one town. This moving about weakens feelings of belonging and encourages a sense of personal loneliness and frustration. Because the school is inextricably entwined in patterns of culture with one of its functions being to transmit the cultural heritage, a portion of the responsibility for helping to encourage a personal sense of worth and belonging for individuals belongs to the schools. For many years, schools have worked in this area; but, as the cultural values change in the society, so the emphasis of the school is forced to change. Leavitt, in discussing curriculum balance in the social scene, summarized his thoughts in the following manner:

. . . There are two steps in counterbalancing the social forces impinging upon the school. The first is to produce the power, which in this case is the knowledge that derives from the disciplined and rigorous study of the society. Armed with this knowledge the school can, either through its students or directly, take a second step, which is to bring to bear upon the society the power it possesses. The alternative to this process is surrender to the web of culture and the surrender of much freedom of action. If, however, the search for the good life requires more freedom with which to seek goals directly, then the production of countervailing power is imperative.[10]

The study of society must become an integral part of curriculums at all levels of schooling. A good starting point in helping youth to understand that many patterns of our culture are common to all persons would be to show the common wants and needs of all men. These needs have been stated in various ways by many sociologists and cultural anthropologists. Brameld states them as follows:

1. Most people do not want to be hungry; they cherish the value of sufficient nourishment.
2. Most people do not want to be cold or ragged; they cherish the value of adequate dress.
3. Most people do not want uncontrolled exposure either to the elements or to people; they cherish the value of shelter and privacy.
4. Most people do not want celibacy; they cherish the value of sexual expression.
5. Most people do not want illness; they cherish the value of physiological and mental health.
6. Most people do not want chronic economic insecurity; they cherish the value of steady work, steady income.
7. Most people do not want loneliness; they cherish the value of companionship, mutual devotion, belongingness.
8. Most people do not want indifference; they cherish the value of recognition, appreciation, status.
9. Most people do not want constant monotony, routine, or drudgery; they cherish the value of novelty, curiosity, variation, recreation, adventure, growth, creativity.

[10]Howard Leavitt, "Curriculum Balance in the Current Social Scene," *Balance in the Curriculum* (Washington: Association for Supervision and Curriculum Development, 1961), p. 32.

10. Most people do not want ignorance; they cherish the value of literacy, skill, information.
11. Most people do not want to be continually dominated; they cherish the value of participation, sharing.
12. Most people do not want bewilderment; they cherish the value of fairly immediate meaning, significance, order, direction.[11]

If one can assume that these basic wants and needs are common to all cultures, then educators have the beginning of a solid foundation to use in explaining the commonality of all men and all cultures. To be sure, there are differences in the methods men use to satisfy their basic needs, but most of these are caused by differences in means available and geographic location. Leavitt comments on the satisfaction of basic needs as a goal of education:

... The purpose of education is to transmit the culture. If culture is conceived as the composite attempt of a people to satisfy basic needs, then the school's role is to transmit to the young that society's accumulation of best ways of satisfying these needs. By making explicit the values or needs toward which society has always been more or less unconsciously moving, the people might at long last state with authority and conviction that the goals of education in its broad sense should be the fullest satisfaction of these needs.[12]

It is often said that man's greatest problem in the twentieth century is man himself. In his personal relations with his family, his neighbors, his business or professional associates, his God, his country, and the world, man needs to come to grips with himself. Educators can help in man's quest for personal meaning and satisfactory, mutually rewarding relationships with other men. They cannot do it alone, and they should not attempt to do so, for this quest must be a communal endeavor with participation by all members of the community. Those who plan future curriculums may well use man's quest for meaning and his search for satisfying personal relationships as the adhesive to hold the curriculums together.

[11]Theodore Brameld, *Toward a Reconstructed Philosophy of Education*, (New York: Holt, Rinehart, and Winston, Inc., 1956), pp. 115–116.
[12]Leavitt, "Curriculum Balance," p. 26.

SUGGESTED READINGS

Brameld, Theodore. *Toward a Reconstructed Philosophy of Education.* New York: Holt, Rinehart, and Winston, Inc., 1956.

Bruner, Jerome S. *The Process of Education.* Cambridge: Harvard University Press, 1961.

Callahan, Raymond E. *Education and the Cult of Efficiency.* Chicago: The University of Chicago Press, 1962.

Clift, Virgil A., Anderson, Archibald W., and Hullfish, H. Gordon, eds. *Negro Education in America.* New York: Harper & Brothers, 1962.

Conant, James B. *The American High School Today.* New York: McGraw-Hill Book Company, Inc., 1959.

———. *Education in the Junior High School Years.* Princeton: Educational Testing Service, 1960.

———. *Slums and Suburbs.* New York: McGraw-Hill Book Company, Inc., 1961.

Ehlers, H., ed. *Crucial Issues in Education.* New York: Henry Holt and Company, 1955.

Fraser, Dorothy M. *Current Curriculum Studies in Academic Subjects.* Washington: National Education Association, 1962.

Giles, H. Harry. *The Integrated Classroom.* New York: Basic Books, Inc., 1959.

Hanna, Paul R. "A National Curriculum Commission for Curriculum Research and Development," *Phi Delta Kappan,* XLII (June 1961), pp. 331-338.

Hodenfield, G. K., and Stinnett, T. M. *The Education of Teachers.* Englewood Cliffs, N. J.: Prentice-Hall, Inc., 1961.

Leavitt, Howard. "Curriculum Balance in the Current Social Scene" *Balance in the Curriculum.* Washington: Association for Supervision and Curriculum Development, 1961.

Lieberman, M. *Education as a Profession.* Englewood Cliffs, N. J.: Prentice-Hall, Inc., 1956.

Noar, Gertrude. *Teaching and Learning the Democratic Way.* Englewood Cliffs, N. J.: Prentice-Hall, Inc., 1963.

Passow, A. Harry, ed. *Education in Depressed Areas.* New York: Teachers College, Columbia University, 1963.

Phi Delta Kappan, XLV (May 1964).

Solomon, Jack, Jr. *Federal Aid to Education.* Lincolnwood, Ill.: National Textbook Corporation, 1961.

Teacher Supply and Demand in Public Schools, 1962. Washington: Research Division, National Education Association, 1962.

VII

VALUES: AN ESSENTIAL FOUNDATION FOR CURRICULUM BUILDING

In almost all competent curriculum literature, values are indicated as one of the most solid bases for curriculum building. An attempt will be made in this chapter to define this idea and to illustrate it, so that educators who wish to experiment with values as a foundation for curriculum design may be able to do so.

The word *values* in its most common connotation leads one to think in terms of right or wrong, good or evil. Writers in the fields of religion, philosophy, and ethics normally use it with a moral connotation. Although this connotation is very vital to public education, here we must also think of the democratic values that we attempt to inculcate in pupils; for example, the concept that under our legal system every man is innocent until he is proven guilty.

Many professional educators, philosophers, religious, military, literary, and civic leaders have suggested a value-oriented core for the education of youth. These leaders agree that the real, lasting results of an education are the commitments which the student carries out of the educative experience into his life to become governing factors in his everyday pattern of living and behavior. As Phenix points out:

The essence of the curriculum—whether considered formally in schools or informally in other agencies of education—consists not of the objective lessons to be learned or courses to be passed, but of the scheme of values, ideals, or life goals which are mediated through the materials of instruction. The really significant outcome of education is the set of governing commitments, the aims of living, that the learner develops. The various subjects of study are simply means for the communication and the appropriation of these values.[1]

Phenix also expresses a conviction that neither the subject-centered nor the progressive school provided an adequate basis for making decisions about the curriculum:

The traditional formal schools taught subjects—the three R's and their higher elaborations. The progressive schools were concerned more with the individual child's interests and needs. The premise of this study is that neither the organized subject fields nor the psychology of personality furnishes the criteria for deciding the content of instruction. The clue to choice lies in the demands that are imposed by the development of modern civilization.[2]

In the succeeding development of ideas, Phenix suggests the thesis that "education is a moral enterprise, where the term *moral* refers to purposeful conduct based on consideration of values."[3] The use of moral in this frame of reference appears to be worth considerable thought and effort in curriculum building by present and future educators. Educating youth for "the good life" has historically been a major concern of curriculum builders, from Plato's time to the present. Although the concept of the good life has changed to meet the times, and the definition of it is hard to agree upon, the goal of teaching it to youth remains.

DEFINITION OF VALUES

Among other dictionary definitions, one may find the following definition of *values*:

[1]Philip H. Phenix, *Education and the Common Good: A Moral Philosophy of the Curriculum* (New York: Harper and Brothers, 1961), p. 18.
[2]*Ibid.*, p. 4.
[3]*Ibid.*, p. 4.

A principle, quality or the like which is regarded as instrinsically desirable; e. g. To value honor above riches. To value personal integrity above fame.[4]

From this simple, direct definition, one begins to get a feeling for the educational, moral, and spiritual meaning of the word. It is from this point of view that the educator needs to look at curriculum design and curriculum building.

Today, much lip service is given to principles, but there is not enough implementation of them in daily living. The public schools, as a bulwark of democracy, are in a favored position to help educate youth in basic principles of daily living. The time has come for educators, parents, youth leaders, churches, and governmental agencies to work together to help young people grow up with a consistent, solid core of *basic values* and *basic principles*. Upon such a foundation, one builds not only better curriculums but better citizens.

Such qualities as tolerance, respect for individual differences, fairness, equality of treatment, a sense of humor, respect for subject-matter knowledge, and a deep abiding reverence for learning itself are transmitted by teachers to pupils. Simply stated, we must acknowledge that the value system of a teacher is what the pupil carries with him permanently. Even though the subject-matter content may be lost, the outstanding teacher's value system remains.

One of the basic purposes of teaching is to effect changed behavior. To help a youngster grow and mature, to help him put service to mankind above personal gain, to help him learn how to live successfully with others, to help him gain the skills and knowledge to earn a living, and to help him find his own place in society are *some* of the goals of teachers. Teachers who are personally successful in attaining these goals use values as the core of their teaching.

DIFFERENT PUPILS HAVE DIFFERENT VALUES

A public-school teacher teaches all the children of all the people. What this means is that public schools should welcome *all* children from *all types* of homes and backgrounds.

[4] *Webster's Unabridged Dictionary*, 2nd ed., (Springfield, Mass.: G. C. Merriam Co., 1959).

The diversity of our citizens makes the task of public education a gigantic one, since each cultural group has its own value system. Despite the heterogeneous public-school population and the different values of diverse national and social groups, teachers have attempted to instill common values for democratic citizenship. Some success has been evident, for most American citizens understand their rights and privileges in a democracy, although they do not always exercise them.

Numerous difficulties are encountered by teachers as they attempt to teach values to their pupils. Many of these problems stem from differences among groups within the community and the school. Examples of such problems, with which teachers must deal, are:

a. A compelling need for immediate rewards as against future-oriented rewards.
b. Preferences for physical solutions to disagreements rather than peaceful discussion.
c. Lack of motivation for the importance of schooling in relation to future personal and economic success.
d. Desire to find success and status outside the framework of the school.
e. Rebellion against female-dominated environment of the school, particularly at the elementary and junior-high levels.
f. A revolt by young males against more mature and academically successful females in the same class at school.
g. A deep sense of isolation and unacceptability as a member of the school and its social groups.

The existence of social classes and the effects of them on pupils and teachers have been well documented in numerous sociological studies.[5]

Consider, for a moment, your own school system and the variety of backgrounds represented by the pupils in it. What would you do, if you were a teacher faced with the problem of teaching values to these pupils? How would you decide which values are important? Would you select thrift as one of the primary values to teach? During

[5]For specific examples see August B. Hollingshead, *Elmtown's Youth* (New York: John Wiley and Sons, 1949), and Robert H. Havighurst, *et al.*, *Growing Up in River City* (New York: John Wiley & Sons, 1962).

the twenties, thirties, and forties, one would probably have answered in the affirmative. Today, after a long period of high wages and inflation, is thrift still a primary value? Today's children grow up from infancy with an "image of opulence" presented to them by the advertising world as the most desirable goal of successful living. Could you fight the impact upon pupils of radio, television, newspapers, magazines, and motion pictures? If you felt that you could overcome these influences, where would you start?

The advertising and communications media are strong influences upon growing children today, so powerful that pupils enter school with a built-in image of life that is not always realistic or accurate. The classroom teacher who would teach values has to undo many undesirable concepts before he can begin to build those that can be of lasting worth. In many cases the fight is too hard, takes too much time and energy from other teaching duties, and consequently is neglected. To many teachers, the built-in concepts children bring to school appear too formidable to overcome.

SUGGESTIONS FOR TEACHING VALUES

The first necessary ingredient in the personality of the teacher who would teach values is courage. It takes great courage to go against the tide of popular thinking and common practice. It is far easier to agree that the teaching of values should be left to the home and church, that the domain of values is outside the province of the school. Where the responsibility really lies, of course, is with all three institutions: the home, the church, and the school. In the days when the "spare the rod and spoil the child" theory was in vogue, the school, church, and home mutually reinforced each other. Although that theory is no longer considered conducive to healthy personality development, the principle of mutual reinforcement by home, church, and school is still sound.

A second but equally important ingredient in the personality of teachers of values is strong commitment to sound democratic, ethical, and moral principles. Since one's value system determines, to a very large extent, one's behavior patterns in relation to other persons, teachers need a deep sense of commitment in order to communicate values to pupils. Basically, this characteristic may be described in terms of behaving in a way which shows that behavior is activated and motivated by belief. In simple language, such behavior on the part of teachers of values implies to pupils that the teacher is as good as his word. Only when pupils feel reasonably sure that teachers believe what they practice can it become possible for them to transfer learned values into their activities in the classroom. The best way for pupils to internalize their educational experiences is to see the teacher in action. For example, the teacher who believes in democratic principles of self-government must make opportunities for pupil-participation and pupil-sharing of classroom responsibilities.

There have been many inevitable shifts and changes in values. For instance, contemporary youthful society no longer places a primary emphasis upon the value of hard work and its rewards. Business and industrial concerns that are in short supply of skilled personnel have often committed themselves to satisfying the immature adolescent dream of considerable authority and prestige with a minimum of responsibility. The times in which we live have conspired to extend beyond reasonable limits the period of dependency of youth. Instead of being motivated by the challenge of taking a risk now so that success may be achieved later, many young persons seeking employment today prefer a guarantee of security. Formerly, most young persons were anxious to do all the work at the bottom of the ladder of success so that they might later climb to a higher, more comfortable position. Vacations and other fringe benefits used to be considered relatively unimportant. Today prospective employees put great emphasis on such matters and place a high value upon leisure. An important question that needs investigation concerns the use made of the increasing amounts of leisure time now available to people.

With many traditional values undergoing shifts and changes, it becomes increasingly difficult for young people to find adults with whom to identify. More than in any other way, values are learned by identification with models. By providing adequate models with whom pupils can identify as they struggle to find themselves and their place in society, the school can offer more aid to youth than can any other public agency in our society. To be adequate for this job, today's teachers must have respect for values and customs of groups other than those of the middle-class American. Many studies document the finding that teachers have predominantly middle-class value systems and that they tend to reject behavior on the part of their pupils that deviates from the middle-class standards.[6] Yet, if teachers are to be adequate models with whom youth can identify in building better value systems, they must be willing to accept and honor differences in childrens' values.

The values that any child brings to school are those that he has learned in the home, the community, or from his peers. It is from this point that the teacher must proceed. Some values may need reinforcing, while others may need to be discarded and replaced by more desirable ones. For example, values such as worship of easy money, the desire for *immediate* satisfaction of wants with no regard for others, and lack of any commitment to a set of moral and ethical principles would be considered undesirable by most teachers. Replacement of undesirable values is a slow and time-consuming process, and great patience is required on the part of the teacher who attempts to help a pupil accomplish such a change. The rewards that may come as a result of such value replacement offer great satisfaction to the teacher who is willing and able to take the risk.

In learning to accept and understand differences in our own culture, we may open the way for acceptance of differences in other cultures. As our world grows increasingly smaller, students must learn to understand and accept cultural differences as well as cultural similarities. Fannie Shaftel has commented that:

Historically, every group has looked with suspicion, and usually with rejection, upon people who are different from themselves. Now, the threat of nuclear warfare and the progress of a worldwide industrial explosion make it necessary for us to understand

[6]For an example see W. Allison Davis, "The Motivation of the Underprivileged Worker" in *Industry and Society*, ed. William Foote Wythe (New York: McGraw-Hill, 1946), pp. 84–106.

and accept one another. This is a time that is both awful and wonderful in its threat and its promise. Scientific advances that enabled us to develop nuclear weapons also make available a technology that can raise the level of all peoples of the earth from mere survival to adequate and creative dimensions. And this we must do to survive. It is an irony of fate that in order to avert catastrophic world war, we must bend every effort to realizing a truly humane society.[7]

It would be difficult to find a more worthy or more practical goal than cross-cultural understanding and acceptance.

THE INDIVIDUAL, THE CURRICULUM, AND VALUES

For many years in American public education, much emphasis has been given to the development of the individual. From the "progressivists" to the core curriculum adherents and the life-adjustment group, educational thinkers and curriculum designers have been concerned with individual growth and development. More often than not, the machinery of curriculum has blocked the attainment of their desired objectives.

Far too many curriculum plans have placed major stress upon one aspect of the pupil's learning. Research in the areas of human growth and personality development indicates that individuals grow and develop on several fronts simultaneously. As Herrick suggests, while discussing values as an area of concern in curriculum development:

> The choice or decision areas of the learning-teaching-curriculum become important focal points for relating and developing the necessary components of any thoughtful, constructive curriculum planning. It seems impossible on the basis of this thinking, then, to have programs of intellectual education, emotional education, or value education. Any kind of significant purposeful behavior action on the part of a human being will always involve all three.[8]

[7]Fannie R. Shaftel, "Values in a World of Many Cultures," *Educational Leadership*, 18 (May 1961), 489.
[8]Herrick, "Sources," p. 66.

Since the child develops and grows in all three areas mentioned in the reference above, the curriculum needs to incorporate all areas simultaneously. Who is to say that any one area of human development is more important than another? Who is to say that a curriculum design should exclude one area of human development while it concentrates on another? To be effective, curriculum designs must include all areas of human development and provide for continuity within them. A neglected area of pupil development upon which greater emphasis is needed concerns the emotional life of pupils. Since we need this increased emphasis upon emotional life as vital to learning, the incorporation of the teaching of values would seem to be one of the surest ways to effect such an accent on modern learning processes.

When children come to school, they bring certain values with them. By observing their actions, it is often possible to perceive their values. One pupil desires to dominate the group. Another wishes to share the leadership. A third is disinterested and withdraws from any group activity. Most all children, however, come to school with a sincere, buoyant interest and strong motivation to learn. Learning to the first-grader is an exciting new experience, one in which he generally wishes to participate wholeheartedly. His desire is so keen that it reflects in his face and his action. What can the school do to nurture this inherent eagerness for learning and to maintain it?

Numerous suggestions have been made by many different educational leaders. One of the most recent is contained in the Trump Plan[9] for more effective utilization of staff time and talent. In addition to suggested reorganization of the time patterns for students and staff in the secondary schools—suggestions that include large group-small group sectioning, individual class schedules for pupils, teaching teams, master teachers, and the liberal use of audio-visual aids for large group presentations—a third aspect of the recommendations deserves close attention. This aspect concerns what is labeled "Individual Study." Individual study would encourage the pupil to assume a much greater share of the responsibility for his own learning. If curriculum planners were willing to operate on the assumption that a major portion of the responsibility for learning

[9] J. Lloyd Trump and Dorsey Baynham, *Focus on Change: Guide to Better Schools* (Chicago: Rand McNally and Company, 1961).

belongs to each individual pupil, then it would seem possible to create public education that has balance, purpose, depth, and utility. Much of the difficulty in today's schools with disciplinary matters and lack of interest and motivation on the part of pupils can be directly traced to a lack of willingness to credit pupils with some intelligence and some ability to make decisions and operate on them. Naturally, some of the decisions pupils make will be less than desirable from the staff viewpoint; yet, some of the most permanent learning comes about as a result of mistakes in judgment.

Pupils need the freedom to make errors that are their own and to learn to live with the consequences or to make a fresh approach. Teachers and administrators do not need to have all the answers, pre-packaged and ready to apply to each pupil dilemma. Freedom to make mistakes, to take responsibility for a large portion of their own learning, and to use teachers and administators as resource persons could make education an exciting, rewarding experience. With excitement in the learning process and challenge in the content and methods, many problems of today's school can be resolved.

EVIDENCE OF A NEED FOR VALUES

When one examines the behavior patterns of pupils in today's schools, it becomes apparent that many of them lack adequate values as guides to thinking and action. In almost all classrooms, on all levels of public education, there are signs of the need for value development. How many pupils appear to have no anchor in their daily life in school or at home? Do some pupils show apathy, listlessness, domineering and aggressive tendencies, shyness and withdrawal, inability to see a job through, resentment toward the teacher and school in general, hostile behavior toward other pupils and persons in positions of authority? These are only a few of the behavioral tendencies that are often symptomatic of a pupil's need for help in the formation of a value system.

Apparent lack of caring by a pupil in several facets of his school life should lead the teacher to consider if his behavior may be related to an inadequate system of values. Behavior that is normally categorized by the terms "problem child" and "juvenile delinquent" may stem from the lack of a value system that motivates socially desirable behavior. Though the school cannot complete the task by itself, it can assist such children in value formation.

TEACHING VALUES: THE NEXT STEP

The first step toward incorporating values into the curriculum is to decide which values the school desires for its pupils. In making this decision, the level of schooling—elementary, junior high, senior high, or college—should be carefully considered, for certain values are more suitable to one level than to another. The next step is to survey the values held by pupils in the school system. This may be accomplished in a number of ways, such as projective techniques, unfinished story techniques, close observation of pupils, anecdotal records of pupils, narrative records kept by teachers of class discussions, and written papers on attitudes, interests, and beliefs. When the school staff has decided which values are most appropriate for a given age or developmental level and the survey of pupils' values has been completed, then the staff is ready to start planning the curriculum.

Though emphasizing values as basic to learning is not a new idea, the idea as presented here consists of looking at our problems in a different way. It is proposed that we try to look at the real values and the underlying motivation of behavior. It is also suggested that, if we do build our new curriculums on a basic foundation of teachers' and pupils' values, we are on the road to functional learning. Each generation of educators has attempted to reach the youth of its time. Each generation has contributed a worth-while amount of insight into learning and pupil behavior. The most pressing task of the present generation of educators involves the proper blending of the heritage of the past and the discoveries of the present and the future. With the rapid expansion of knowledge and technology and the shifting of social habits and norms, a curriculum based on values offers the brightest outlook for educating the youth of America.

If we are to decrease the number of cafeteria-type educational programs and help pupils to learn to care and to care deeply enough to act, we need to look at curriculum building from a new perspective. Education began with its main objective as learning to think. During the days of progressive education and its greatest impact in this country, a second aspect was emphasized: learning by doing. Today, we need the third and most vital aspect added to our thinking and doing processes—that of learning to feel. Through the development of value systems, we can put feeling in its proper place as the motivator of action. Through the combination of intelligent thought, deep feeling, and action based on thought and feeling, many problems will lend themselves to resolution. A happy and successful combination of thinking, feeling, and action offers the best hope for the development of the kind of leadership so desperately needed in today's world.

SUGGESTED READINGS

Allport, Gordon, and Vernon, Philip. *Study of Values*. New York: Houghton Mifflin Co., 1951.

Corey, Fay L. *Values of Future Teachers*. New York: Columbia University Press, 1955.

Dahlke, H. Otto. *Values in Culture and Classroom*. New York: Harper & Brothers, 1958.

Educational Policies Commission. *Moral and Spiritual Values in the Public School*. Washington: National Education Association, 1951.

Fleming, Robert S., ed. *Curriculum for Today's Boys and Girls*. Columbus, Ohio: Charles E. Merrill Books, Inc., 1963.

Fox, Robert S. "Curriculum Development with a Purpose," *Theory Into Practice*, I (October 1962), 202–207.

Getzels, Jacob W. "The Acquisition of Values in School and Society" in *The High School in a New Era*. Chicago: University of Chicago Press, 1958, pp. 146–161.

Ginzberg, Eli, ed. *Values and Ideals of American Youth*. New York: Columbia University Press, 1961.

Havighurst, Robert, and Taba, Hilda. *Adolescent Character and Personality*. New York: John Wiley and Sons, 1949.

Pritzkau, Philo T. *Dynamics of Curriculum Improvement*. Englewood Cliffs, N. J.: Prentice-Hall, Inc., 1959.

Thelen, Herbert A. *Education and the Human Quest*. New York: Harper & Brothers, 1960.

Zirbes, Laura. *Focus of Values in Elementary Education*. New York: G. P. Putnam's Sons, 1960.

VIII

ARTICULATION: A PRESSING NEED FOR BETTER CURRICULUMS

Curriculum building has, unfortunately, generally been a matter of taking one tiny segment of a school system and attempting to improve this small segment with little or no relationship to the entire educational effort. A third grade, in one of several elementary schools in a district, experiments with a new reading program. Other third-grade teachers in other elementary schools in the system usually know of the new work, but fifth-and sixth-grade teachers are seldom aware of it. Furthermore, the junior and senior high-school teachers know nothing about the trial program and, even if they were informed, would probably feel it had little or no connection with their teaching. In most instances, attempts to improve the curriculum have been isolated in one phase of a program or in one school in a system. Communication has been poor or nonexistent, and results of new ventures have never been made available to the total teaching personnel of the system. The net result of such poor communication has been little real curriculum improvement in many school systems.

Gone are the days when educators can continue to pass the buck to a progressively lower level of educational experience, as illustrated by the following rhyme:

Passing It On

The College President:
"Such rawness in a student is a shame
But lack of preparation is to blame."

The High School Principal:
> "Good heav'ns, what crudity! The boy's a fool.
> The fault, of course, is with the grammar school."

The Grammar School Principal:
> "Oh, that from such a dunce I might be spared!
> They send them up to me so unprepared."

The Primary Principal:
> "Poor kindergarten blockhead! And they call
> That preparation! Worse than none at all."

The Kindergarten Teacher:
> "Never such lack of training did I see.
> What sort of person can the mother be!"

The Mother:
> "You stupid child! But then you're not to blame
> Your father's family are all the same."[1]

Anonymous

The rhyme expresses more truth than poetry; for many years, this type of thinking has been used as an excuse for poor pupil performance. Actually one very simple reason for lack of success may well be lack of curricular articulation from one level of schooling to the next.

How can we obtain better results from efforts to improve curriculum? An immediate step that most school systems can take consists of a systematic attempt to articulate their instructional programs.

MEANING OF ARTICULATION

What does *articulation* mean in its educational usage? In simple, nontechnical language it means "the unification and coordination of learning experiences." To articulate a curriculum demands that a school system examine it thoroughly, delete parts that are no longer useful, add new content where it is needed, eliminate unnecessary

[1]John T. Wahlquist, *An Introduction to American Education* (New York: The Ronald Press, 1947), pp. 232–233.

duplication, extend the continuity of the curriculum, and revise both method and content where it appears feasible. When a program of articulation is well done, there is continuity of learning experiences throughout the school system, from kindergarten through the senior year in high school. There is reason and logic applied to the examination of the system's program of studies, co-curricular activities, athletic programs, cultural and aesthetic programs, citizenship activities, and community service functions. After a study to articulate the curriculum, teachers and administrators at all levels of schooling begin to see how their individual efforts fit into the total picture of public education in their community.

Building a curriculum is much like building a house. To insure a well-built house, one begins with a solid foundation. So it is with curriculum building, for a solid foundation is the most certain way to insure that the continuing learning experiences at each succeedingly higher level will have depth and meaning for the pupil.

Although it would seem relatively simple for a group of teachers and administrators working in the same school system to arrive at a thorough understanding of the entire educational program, in reality this is much more difficult than it appears. Teachers have different backgrounds and interests that affect what they teach and how they teach it; they have had diverse programs of preparation. Although some teachers have had experience with the importance of developmental patterns in relation to the learning process, others have had heavy emphasis upon subject matter to be taught, to the neglect of the study of children's developmental processes. The primary teacher may only be able to see and feel the dependence patterns of young children in her classroom. The junior-high teacher may only understand the natural ebullience of the seventh- , eighth- , and ninth-graders. The senior-high teacher may only be able to see the vital importance of more and more subject matter for youngsters who will soon be at work or in college. When a school system attempts to get teachers of all levels together to work on a common in-service program, many differences of opinion and interests occur. If one is to achieve a well-articulated curriculum, the starting point is found with teachers and administrators attempting to reach a measure of agreement on basic objectives, purposes, and goals of the entire public-school program.

In addition to being systemwide in many school districts, articulation is a problem that is nationwide. The children of this generation are a part of a highly mobile population as will be children of coming generations. Children may move from one section of the country to another several times during their years of public schooling, and they have a right to a reasonable degree of continuity of learning. One suggested solution to this problem is the creation of a national curriculum commission, nongovernmental in nature.[2] Such a commission could provide some basis for continuity and, at least to some extent, would provide a national common core of values, attitudes, knowledge, and skills that our public schools should give their pupils.

SOCIAL ARTICULATION AND SUBJECT-MATTER ARTICULATION

In discussing the pressing need for articulation of instructional programs, one should point out that the public schools have done a creditable piece of work in the area of social articulation. Great strides have been made in the past twenty years with regard to this side of the pupil's school life. Teachers and administrators, with the assistance of guidance personnel, have helped to make the transition from one level of schooling to another much less rigid than it was formerly. In general, social articulation has been well planned and well executed. Programs of visitation within a school system, such as the sixth graders visiting the junior high school preparatory to entering, have become common and have been very successful.

The real difficulty, as James Conant points out, has come with the lack of coordination of the curriculum:

Often an excellent social transition is provided for pupils between one school and another in the same system, but too often there is a failure to coordinate subject-matter instruction between

[2]Paul R. Hanna, "Curriculum and Instruction," *National Education Association Journal*, 52 (January 1963), 52–54.

schools and between grades even in the same school. Without question, I consider the lack of what educators call articulation one of the most serious problems in many school systems.[3]

Although Conant's comment is directed specifically at the junior high school, the same criticism can be applied to the elementary and the senior high schools.

COMMUNICATION AS A WAY TO BETTER ARTICULATION

An immediate way in which most school systems could improve the articulation of curriculums lies in the improvement of existing patterns of communications and the creation of new ones. If an individual school is fairly small, small enough so that all the teachers can get together and exchange frequent reports on their activities, the problem of clearer communications is lessened. The national trend, however, is toward larger schools. As school consolidation moves forward, the small rural school moves closer to oblivion. Probably as well articulated a program of studies as one could desire used to exist in the one-room country school. Since the teacher had several grades in one room and a small number of pupils, she knew firsthand how each phase of the curriculum should be dovetailed into the succeeding one. She also knew every pupil, his strengths as well as his weaknesses.

What can be done in the larger schools to improve patterns of communication among staff members and between the administration and the teaching staff? How can the principal of a school with forty to eighty teachers communicate with them clearly and adequately? What can he do to reach his staff so that his ideas will be understood and assimilated? Is a group of forty to eighty too large to reach by personal communication? Can such a staff be subdivided into smaller groups where face-to-face communication can operate at a maximum level of efficiency? What kind of oral and written communication stands the best chance of being well utilized by such a staff?

[3]James B. Conant, *A Memorandum to School Boards: Recommendations for Education in the Junior High School Years* (Princeton: Educational Testing Service, 1960), p. 33.

Questions such as these need to be answered in order to understand the best possible approach to clear communication.

In the first place, an administrator with a large staff must realize that there is no substitute for face-to-face situations when he can talk with his staff, and he should save time for individual conferences. In addition, he will need to communicate with them by intercom and in writing through a daily announcement bulletin. The ways in which the administrator communicates with his faculty are important to him and to them. There are times when the message should be short and direct. At other times much more detail and explanation will be necessary.

LEADERSHIP: AN ESSENTIAL ELEMENT

If a school district is to achieve a high measure of articulation in its curriculum, positive leadership is necessary. Although the leadership should come from within the system—and indeed it must for the sake of continuity of the program—direction is often best obtained from an outside consultant. Such a consultant may usually be found at a regional or local university or college. The objective viewpoint brought into the local system by a consultant enables school personnel to see their problems in a light that is impossible when one is involved in the outcome. The consultant has no real involvement in the outcome: his role is primarily one of stimulator, resource person, coordinator of the group efforts, and facilitator in terms of obtaining special help for specific subject-matter teachers. Subject-matter specialists—often available on the consultant's own campus—can be brought into the local school situation whenever they are needed. Although the major responsibility for the conduct of the school system's articulation program rests with the general consultant, help in a specific area is normally obtained from a specialist in that area.

The responsibility for *initiating* a program of articulation of curriculum rests with the local school administrator. In most cases, the district superintendent is the man who gives the impetus to such a study. The superintendent can, through an optimistic outlook toward an articulation program, set a tone with his staff from the outset. The fact that the top administrative leader has a firm belief in the success of the study will tend to encourage a similar attitude on the part of the participating teachers.

The entire school district needs to be a part of an articulation program, because all are affected by it. Participation by all teachers through representative committees offers one way to organize such a large group of teachers efficiently. Since all levels of public schools within the district should be involved, committees will need to be made up on both a horizontal and a vertical basis. Some committees will be in subject-matter areas from elementary school through senior high school. Other committees will need to cut across traditional subject-matter lines and look at the district pattern of general education, while still others will look at the patterns of special education.

PLANNING FOR ARTICULATION

Good articulation of curriculum must be carefully planned, and allowances should be made for staff to have available school time in the planning stage of the program. To begin the planning stage of such a program it is helpful to have a long, hard look at present practices; one needs to start by examining all the learning currently going on in the school district. A sound starting point may be found in a teacher survey of each classroom in the system. Asking teachers how well satisfied they are with current content and method may offer clues to improvement of continuity. Classroom teachers know better than anyone else whether the material they are teaching and the methods they are using really reach the pupils and satisfy their needs. When teachers have the opportunity to look at what they are doing, and the time necessary to do it in somewhat more than cursory fashion, they often have suggestions to offer that make for an improved curriculum.

Some school systems have found that careful examination of the entire curriculum proceeds best by approaching one subject-matter area at a time. For instance, the first year of the study would be devoted to English; the second year to mathematics; the third to science, and so on throughout all the subject-matter areas. In this way, teachers from all grade levels can work together on the same general topic: e.g., How can the teaching of English be improved and articulated from grades 1-12? Questions can be asked and answers can be found to remove unnecessary duplications, to include more varied experiences in the program, and to make the subject matter more appropriate to the age and maturity levels of the pupils. In a thorough re-examination of what is being done, teachers may find that the interests of pupils at different levels can be used to develop more functional units within an area of study. The results of the teacher survey of present practices may be used as one of the criteria upon which to base better articulation.

Another approach consists of a sampling of the parents of school-age children in terms of their satisfactions with the present program. Do parents think the schools are teaching all the necessary subjects to children? Do the parents feel that one aspect of the curriculum is being neglected while another is being overemphasized? How do the parents feel about the amount of homework given by the teachers? How do parents feel that they can best help achieve the objectives of the school? Are the educational objectives of the school and those of the parents reasonably similar? How can the school and the parents work together more closely to benefit the child? These and similar questions can give the school some insight into how the parents feel and provide some leads toward establishing better articulation. Such a sampling of parent opinion may also tend to improve the school's public relations in the community, and an improved position may lead to stronger and more energetic support for planned change in curriculum.

A source of information that is often overlooked lies in the pupil population itself. Who else knows better whether the curriculum is serving them to its best ability? To ascertain whether a specific method of teaching or a specific amount of content is doing the job it was intended to do, one needs to ask the pupil. The pupil, after all, is the person for whom the entire educational enterprise has been planned, and if it does not serve him as well as was hoped, he should be the first to know. His ability to isolate at least the more imme-diate or short-range goals should be utilized. Questions asked pupils about relationships between one grade or year and the next might help pinpoint gaps in the program. Because recent graduates can usually assess quite accurately the strengths and weaknesses of the curriculum, another worth-while survey would involve a followup study of high-school graduates over a five-year period.

With the data supplied by the surveys of parents, pupils, teachers and principals, and recent graduates, the planning committee should be ready to try to create a new approach to the curriculum. From the answers supplied, it may be possible to find the threads to help weave a more adequate, well-coordinated curriculum. It may also be possible to initiate some experimental pilot studies based on re-search findings in learning and human growth and development. These pilot projects could then be measured against traditional prac-tices, and new approaches might well grow out of the comparisons.

Committee Planning Groups

To coordinate the planning of an articulation program several committees are necessary. The first committee selected should be an Advisory Committee. This committee can be made up of the super-intendent, a representative of the board of education, a consultant, several principals representing all levels of instruction, and several classroom teachers elected by the local teachers association. The functions of this group can be mainly those of a clearing house, ap-proval agency, and assigner of priorities to instructional problems that need to be studied.

The next major committee may be called the Articulation Com-mittee and can be chosen from the supervisory and teacher groups of staff members. Representation on this committee may be weighted heavily in favor of the classroom teacher group. The Advisory Committee should select members for this group to cut across sub-ject-matter lines and to bring together both elementary and second-ary teachers. If one wishes to secure maximum output with a mini-mum of loss of time and energy, the size of this committee should not exceed fifteen members. Its function would be to define and describe articulation projects that appear to be most immediate for the school system and to serve as the central information agency for the entire system. It can also plan the overall nature of the sub-projects to be studied and help to coordinate the work of the individual school study committees.

The third committee necessary may be called the Individual School Committee or Study Group. A committee of this type should be formed in each school building in the system. These committees are the ones that gather the data within their own buildings relative to specific areas needing closer coordination and greater continuity. The building principal and a small group of teachers elected by their fellow staff members form the backbone of this committee. It is their responsibility to work on the articulation problem most needing attention in their own building and the transitional problems that occur in the step from their building to the next higher level in the system.

As the Individual School Committees begin to work and study their own immediate problems, it is usual for several building committees to discover that they have common problems. At this point the Articulation Committee may call in representatives of the Study Committees in the individual schools and assign a specific facet of the common problems to each Study Group. Later the Study Groups can put their findings together and make recommendations to the Articulation Committee. The Articulation Committee, in turn, will make recommendations to the Advisory Committee. The Advisory Committee can either accept recommendations and put them into practice in the school system or rule that they go back to the sub-committees for further study.

Good leadership on all of the committees is a prime requisite. Another vital necessity is a means of publication of the work of all committees. To help keep the groups informed of the others' progress and problems, a staff newsletter might be established. If communication breaks down, the chances of success are considerably lessened. Keeping each group informed of the others' work is a stimulant to better morale, and when morale is high, the chances of creative solutions to articulation problems are greatly improved.

RESULTS OF BETTER ARTICULATION

One of the greatest barriers to improved articulation lies in the grade-level organization used in most schools. These grade divisions, artificial lines that keep pupils of a particular age together over the period of a year, usually result in rigid subject-matter organization, with little or no crossing of a grade boundary. Attempts to improve the continuity of learning experiences and to open the areas of study have resulted in the ungraded primary school. An example on the secondary-school level is the "phase learning" program of the Melbourne, Florida, High School. The South Florida Education Center, at Fort Lauderdale, will be ungraded from kindergarten through university level. Such a curriculum plan should lead to a high degree of articulation and may introduce many new concepts into other school systems.

With the removal of grade-line barriers as such, pupils have a better opportunity to enjoy continuity of learning and to carry over parts of one learning experience to the next one. Ungraded elementary schools operate on this theory, as do the secondary schools that have tried to remove the rigid grade divisions.

When articulation is improved among all levels of schooling, from elementary school through college, faculty members of all institutions will have better relationships. Elementary teachers will visit in secondary-school and college classrooms. College staff members and secondary-school teachers will exchange visits with elementary teachers and with each other. Some colleges invite high-school administrators and teachers to come to the campus to visit with their former students. Visits such as these lead toward improved articulation between high school and college, for the college freshman can readily see what his high school did well and what it did not do so well. High school guidance counselors, principals, and teachers can go home with a fairly sound picture of their school's strengths and weaknesses and, hopefully, make necessary changes.

As a result of better articulation there will be better communication, and teachers on all levels will begin to see continuity in education stretching from nursery school through the university level.

Pupils, instead of feeling that their school years are a maze of disjointed learning experiences with no central purpose, will be able to perceive some shape in their educational experiences.

To check on its progress toward better articulation, a school system must do a continuous evaluation of program and learning experiences. Generally speaking, revision of plans represents a very healthy sign of professional growth. As teachers focus their attention upon improved articulation, they become sensitive to pupil needs, and methods and content begin to fall into a realistic, understandable pattern. As more teachers and administrators become aware of the pupils' need for continuity of learning experiences, we can anticipate better articulation throughout the public-school systems.

SUGGESTED READINGS

Association for Supervision and Curriculum Development. *A Look at Continuity in the School Program.* Washington: The Association, 1958.

Briggs, T. H., *et al. Secondary Education.* New York: The Macmillan Company, 1950.

Conant, James B. *Recommendations for Education in the Junior High School Years.* Princeton: Educational Testing Service, 1960.

French, W. M. *American Secondary Education.* New York: The Odyssey Press, 1957.

Hanna, Paul R. "Curriculum and Instruction," *National Education Association Journal,* 52 (January 1963), pp. 52–54.

Stratemeyer, F. B., *et al. Developing a Curriculum for Modern Living.* 2nd ed. New York: Bureau of Publications, Teachers College, Columbia University, 1957.

IX

BARRIERS TO CURRICULUM BUILDING

In spite of the best plans for a curriculum-building program by teachers, administrators, selected pupils, and representative parents, there will be barriers to progress and productivity. Some of the barriers to curriculum building are realistic and practical. Others exist only in the minds of men. Some of these barriers can probably be overcome through cooperative efforts by teachers and administrators. Others may require a re-educative process for citizens of the community.

One way to approach these barriers is to assess the importance of curriculum change to the school and its community. Some schools drift along for many years with little or no apparent progress in either academic course content or methods of teaching. Other schools never seem to be satisfied unless they are continually experimenting with materials, content, and methods.

Proposals for curriculum change come from within and without the school system. Social changes in the nation or the world may precipitate local curriculum change. Local or regional business and industrial needs for certain skills may also bring definite changes. Teachers and administrators may ask for the inclusion of new courses or the teaching of old courses with new methods. If the school and its community give top-priority to continuous curriculum improvement programs, then some barriers that exist in less supportive communities will not be found.

WHAT ARE SOME MAJOR BARRIERS?

If we were to ask any group of teachers and administrators what they consider the biggest barriers to building an improved curriculum, we would get some unanimity in the answers. We would probably find the most frequently quoted barrier to be "lack of time to work on curriculum improvement." Another frequently mentioned item would be "lack of instructional materials and money." Another common one is "lack of community interest and support for curriculum change." All three of these reasons are both realistic and practical. Let's examine them one at a time.

LACK OF TIME

Teachers' working days are quite tightly scheduled; practically every moment of each working day is accounted for from 8:00 A.M. till 3:30 P.M. or whatever time school is dismissed. During these hours teachers instruct children, exercise them, listen to their problems, counsel them, collect monies from them, chaperone their lunch hours, and help them plan their future. After school hours, teachers often sponsor clubs and other student activities or have conferences with parents. At night, they often serve as ticket sellers or gatekeepers at athletic or dramatic events. When do they find time to work on curriculum?

Many schools expect teachers and administrators to tackle the job of curriculum improvement after four o'clock in the afternoon. To add to an already full day of demanding responsibility the additional task of creating better learning situations is more than one should ask.

There are several ways in which a school system may free teachers to work on curriculums. One method is to inform the community of the importance of the curriculum study; then dismiss the pupils early one day per month. Most parents are willing to go along with this idea, provided they understand the reason for early dismissal and the importance of the study. Another way in which curriculum study may be encouraged is to lengthen the teaching contract year. Preschool and postschool workshops and conferences often supply the direction and incentive for less energy-consuming curriculum tasks that may be carried on throughout the year. Still another way to provide time is to revise teaching schedules so that teachers who need to work together on curriculum improvement may have a free period together. A final suggestion is for the administration to provide an occasional substitute so that a teacher may use a school day for observation in a neighboring community. Such visits often stimulate teachers to greater interest and action in regard to curriculum improvement, and the ideas gained may often be used in the local program.

In addition to the four listed above, there must be other ways to free teachers for participation in curriculum-improvement activities at times when they are not devoid of energy and enthusiasm.

LACK OF INSTRUCTIONAL MATERIALS AND MONEY

School systems that are financially pressed to the point where they can barely meet the minimum requirements for salaries, buildings, and equipment can hardly expect teachers to be interested in improving the curriculum. To expect teachers and administrative staff members to put time and energy into building better curriculums, the school system must be willing and able to spend monies for equipment, professional study and travel, research projects, and enriching instructional materials. To produce an enriched curriculum requires both broadened and enriched teachers and materials.

Some school systems provide little material beyond the conventional textbook, which may be as much as fifteen years old. Teaching today with only a textbook is like trying to perform surgery with a jackknife. It can be done, but seldom is, except in isolated emergency circumstances. Today's students are accustomed to multidimensional media of instruction. From earliest childhood they see television and become accustomed to the visual approach to learning. Books and magazines as well as motion picture cameras and projectors and slide-film projectors are common in many homes today. The teacher must be able to compete with other visual and auditory media in order to hold pupil interest.

Although the textbook is a very important aid to learning, it is quite sterile as the *only* approach to learning. A curriculum can be tremendously improved through the use of newer instructional materials. Think, for example, of the added dimension given to the study of biology through the use of an overhead projector. Specimens that could only be seen individually through a microscope can now be projected on an enlarged scale for the entire class to view at once. In social studies, relief maps now show elevations, land masses, rivers, lakes, and oceans. The topography comes alive for pupils on two- or three-dimensional representations. This type of instructional aid is a far cry from the old flat map.

Major improvement of curriculums requires the use of some or all of the modern instructional aids. Teachers have a legitimate point when they give the lack of instructional materials and money as a reason for nonparticipation in curriculum-improvement projects. Although many of the new instructional aids are relatively inexpensive, their purchase or rental does require some outlay of money.

Less than adequate financial resources can cause much ill will and lowered morale. If only enough money is available to pay low salaries to the instructional and administrative staffs, little in the way of better curriculums can be expected. Then, too, educators who are overly concerned with financial problems have little interest in devoting much time or thought to curriculum improvement. An improved curriculum requires something more than just the bare financial support. Some extra money needs to be provided in the annual budget, specifically earmarked to support curriculum-building ventures.

LACK OF COMMUNITY INTEREST AND SUPPORT

Because there is such a vast difference between the values of the school and those of the community, some school systems feel that they are islands within the community they serve. If improved public relations are not fostered, in such a community, poor public attitude will be a definite barrier to curriculum improvement. It is always difficult, if not impossible, for educators to move ahead in their thinking and practice without some measure of community understanding, interest, or support.

Communities show their lack of interest and support in several ways. One of the most common is an insistence upon a return by the school to the "fundamentals" and the "3R's." If the public thinks any new change is a step backward, then this attitude serves as a very effective deterrent. One can hardly expect teachers to create new programs only to become victims of severe public criticism. Only a very secure teacher or administrator would be able to go forward with new ideas in the face of continual discouragement. Most school staff members would maintain the status quo and sponsor only those types of learning activity that draw no criticism.

Certain pressure groups in the community may also have a most adverse effect upon curriculum change. Some of these groups have tried hard to restrict instruction in the school to noncontroversial areas; politics and international forms of government are examples of two areas that have often been severely condemned. By applying pressure through speeches, radio, and other news media, these groups have sought to intimidate the teachers and administrators. Sometimes they have succeeded to the point where teachers refuse to try out any new idea that might lead to further intimidation. Attempts by pressure groups to control curriculum content tend to fill the entire educational atmosphere of the school with fear. Once fear takes hold of the teacher's mind and actions, healthy learning activity by pupils ceases, and school becomes a dull, rote kind of repetitious daily experience where the teacher becomes a warden rather than a prospector.

Community members who have not been in close touch with the schools and who do not feel at home in the schools can hardly be expected to be supportive of curriculum change. A major cause of poor relations may be found in faulty communication. It is the responsibility of public-school administrators to open channels of communication between the school and the community. These channels, once opened, should be watched carefully and kept open. School news can be passed along via press, radio, television, news bulletins, workshops, parent-teacher conferences, and open houses at school. If one wants an interested, supportive community, the school must take the leadership in keeping communication open. An informed community is usually a supportive community. One which is uninformed may be either disinterested or extremely aggressive in attacking school policies.

Communication is essentially a two-way street. If it is to be effective, the receiver must have the chance to react and initiate his own answer to the message sent out. Schools need to create cooperative working situations where parents and educators can sit down together and share reactions to suggested curriculum changes. A parent who receives good communication from the school yet completely misunderstands the intent and purpose of the communication may be a real stumbling block in the path of change. If a person feels that he is being discriminated against, it might as well be true. As has often been pointed out, feelings are facts. What one believes to be true might just as well be so, even if the incident is only a figment of his imagination. Good communication calls for face-to-face meetings and person-to-person relationships so that misunderstandings may be corrected before they can cause serious damage.

Another barrier to curriculum improvement that exists primarily in people's minds is reverence for tradition. When this reverence is so compelling that it blocks consideration of new ways, then it stymies all efforts by educators toward progress in curriculum. Parents and other citizens of a particular community may only respect the kind of instructional program that they encountered in their own school days, though this kind of program may be completely outmoded and unrealistic for today's youth. Yet, there are adults who still believe that in order for a school subject to be worth time and study it must be very difficult and distasteful. A carryover from the old formal-discipline theory of learning, this thinking is not applicable to the kinds of learning experiences needed today.

BARRIERS AS TEACHERS SEE THEM

From the teacher's point of view, barriers to curriculum improvement often look different than they do from the viewpoint of the administration or from the viewpoint of professional educators. Here is a list of barriers as the teachers see them.

1. Unprofessional conduct and attitudes within teacher groups.
2. Program did not grow out of teacher's suggestion, but rather from a top administrative suggestion.
3. Teachers wanted grade-level groups which consultants and administration frowned upon.
4. The administration never clearly defined the limits within which teachers could work.
5. Teachers were suspicious of the motives of the consultants and administration.[1]

Doesn't it seem peculiar that not one of the five items in the Fullagar study corresponds to the three items that most educators would list—lack of time, money, and community support? How could a group of teachers see five entirely different barriers? The answer is relatively simple. The teachers in this research sample chose the five barriers that were most important to them in their own communities. Different groups of teachers in different school districts and communities may find barriers that bear little relationship to each other.

One who has had teaching experience can look at the five problems the teachers in the Fullagar study cited as barriers to curriculum improvement and understand why these would appear as trouble spots. One who has not yet had teaching experience can perhaps get "the feel" or atmosphere created by such situations through his reading. Let's look at the first reason given: "unprofessional conduct and attitudes within teacher groups."

What do teachers mean by "unprofessional conduct and attitudes" in teacher groups? The answer to this can be found in the teachers' lounge in most schools. Unfortunately there are some teachers who use their free time to gossip and to criticize their co-workers. Certainly teachers may disagree professionally with fellow teachers or administrators; yet it is highly unprofessional to make public spec-

[1]William A. Fullagar, "Some Teacher-Sensed Problems in Curriculum Improvement" (Unpublished doctoral dissertation, Columbia University, 1951).

tacles of their disagreements. Undisciplined criticism that is motivated more by emotion than by facts can be categorized as unprofessional conduct. Teachers also tend to form cliques within a
faculty of some size, and this often plays one segment of the faculty
against another.

The other four reasons given by teachers indicate a general lack
of trust between the teaching staff and the administrative or con-
sultative staffs. Teachers will resist curriculum change if they feel
they are being used. Such behavior by teachers is almost an instinc-
tive reaction, for they have been manipulated too often in the past.
Most teachers want to participate in the making of decisions that will
vitally affect them and their daily teaching schedules.

Another researcher who went to the teacher to ascertain attitudes
toward curriculum change was Evelyn Banning,[2] who investigated
attitudes among 65 junior-high school teachers in Pittsfield, Massachusetts. Through the use of a questionnaire and structured interview she found that the degree of teacher-favorableness toward
curriculum change was affected by three personal relationships:
teacher-administrator, teacher-pupil, and teacher-community.
Favorableness of attitude toward change correlated significantly
with the teacher's feeling that he was a real participant in the formu-
lation and implementation of curriculum policy. It was also found
that the teachers who had more favorable attitudes toward change
were those who had harmonious relationships with pupils in the
classroom and who were active participants in community life. In
still another study[3] it was found that teachers who had relationships
of an understanding, supportive, or cooperative nature with pupils,
administrators, other teachers, and the community were more ready
for curriculum change than those who had negative feelings in these
areas.

In all these studies the same kinds of potential barriers to curricu-

[2]Evelyn I. Banning, "Teacher Attitudes Toward Curriculum Change, A
Study of the Junior High School Teachers of Pittsfield" (Unpublished doctoral dissertation, Harvard University, 1951).

[3]James K. Duncan, "An Instrument for Measuring Readiness for Curriculum Change" (Unpublished doctoral dissertation, University of Florida,
1954).

lum improvement kept repeating themselves. Again and again, teachers indicated that they felt the need of loyalty and support from those with whom and for whom they worked if they were to feel interested in curriculum change. Otherwise, they were not interested in working extra hours and expending additional energies to assist in curriculum change.

The importance of teachers' feelings is related to Sharp's thesis that "curriculum develops basically as the result of the development of teachers' personalities."[4] If a change in teachers' personalities is a basic factor in curriculum development, then one would expect teachers' feelings to play a major role in such personality development or change. If teachers feel that supportive actions by principals and other staff members are necessary to make them want to change curriculum (and this is precisely what they indicated in the several studies cited) then Sharp's thesis seems valid. Stating this thesis another way, one could say that curriculum changes as teachers' personalities change.

From the data interpretations in the studies cited, it would seem logical to assume that teachers who feel less hostile toward administrators, fellow teachers, pupils, and the community in general would be teachers who affect desirable curriculum change. When teachers have a warm supportive feeling toward the community, pupils, and fellow staff members, major barriers in their minds to curriculum improvement are removed. If we really expect teachers to work hard at building better curriculums, then we must attempt to reduce any feelings of hostility they may have toward the community and the people with whom they work.

As the curriculum leader becomes acquainted with teachers and administrators, he finds that there are two rather distinct groups of persons. First, he finds the recently educated teachers and administrators. Secondly, he finds those teachers and administrators who were educated some years ago and have had a number of years of public school experience. The recently educated group is much more self-directive than the older group. Older programs of teacher

[4]George Sharp, *Curriculum Development as Re-education of the Teacher* (New York: Teachers College, Columbia University, 1951).

education were basically authority-oriented, while the newer programs have emphasized self-decision and independent thinking.[5]

This kind of division of a staff, with the older philosophy versus the newer philosophy, may be a very real barrier. Experience with newer concepts, without being forced to reject older tried methods, may assist the more experienced teacher to modernize his conception of the curriculum. The curriculum leader in this case will need to be a specialist in the re-educative process both on an individual and a group basis. He will also have to help younger and less experienced teachers learn to be tolerant of teachers who are far more dependent on authority than they. Although the curriculum leader is not primarily a counselor, he should be well versed in group processes and counseling techniques. There is little doubt that barriers to curriculum improvement lie in the thinking, practice, and methods of some teachers. Effective work with teachers who need to modernize their thinking and practices may enable them to contribute fully and happily to the improvement of their schools.

A STUDY OF SECONDARY TEACHERS AND BARRIERS

Several years ago, the author investigated a selected sample of one hundred secondary-school teachers in Georgia regarding their feelings about barriers to curriculum improvement. The focus of the study was upon personal and professional relationships between teachers and those with whom they worked closely in their jobs. Attempts were made to assess qualities of relationships between teachers and administrators, teachers and pupils, teachers and fellow staff members, and teachers and parents, which affected both positively and negatively their feelings toward curriculum-improvement activities.[6] In other words, what were the barriers to curriculum improvement contained in close personal and professional relationships connected with teaching?

Although the teachers in the sample were all secondary teachers and the viewpoints they expressed were peculiar to their schools,

[5]*Ibid.*, p. 84.
[6]Cay, dissertation.

their communities, and their relationships, some of the findings could be applied to almost any curriculum-planning program. Here is what teachers who were judged favorable toward curriculum improvement said about their principals:

My principal tries to help in all situations, as he attempts to remove obstacles.

I can discuss all types of school problems with him, and he advises me when asked to do so.

He frequently uses teachers on committees to help plan school affairs.

We always make many suggestions about curriculum improvement and our principal uses them.

Our principal always consults us before assigning any "extra" duties.

He respects our status as a teacher by calling us in for discussion before making decisions which affect us.

Our principal holds at least two social affairs each year, for the teachers, when he acts as host.

He exerts no pressure upon us to join professional groups. It is a matter of personal choice.

Our principal backs us up in all matters of pupil discipline problems.[7]

Teachers who were unfavorable toward curriculum improvement had the following things to say about their relationships with their principals:

He understands discipline problems, but he is very poor in his human relationships.

Our principal is too critical of mistakes of minor importance.

He rarely seeks help from teacher committees in school planning.

Only a selected few of our teachers are ever called in by the principal for discussion of curriculum changes.

[7]*Ibid.*, p. 162.

He usually assigns extra duties without consulting us at all.

Our principal does not support us as he should. The word of a pupil is as good as ours in disciplinary matters.

We have no social affairs where our principal acts as host and entertains us.

He is unwilling to delegate any responsibility to us.

We are never consulted by our principal concerning planning and policy-making decisions.

He lacks understanding of human nature.[8]

Those teachers favorable toward curriculum improvement had the following to say about relationships with fellow teachers:

We have many opportunities for faculty social gatherings, and we thoroughly enjoy them.

I enjoy small group work with other teachers in our school, and we usually accomplish a great deal.

There is no favoritism shown on our faculty. We all feel that we are equally important.

Criticism from other teachers is usually stimulating and helpful to me.

The teachers in our school who lead curriculum improvement work have advanced professional training, understand the pupils' needs, and possess a good professional attitude.

I enjoy discussing new ideas with other teachers, and I usually profit from their viewpoints.

I value constructive criticism from other teachers, and I often analyze my behavior for necessary changes in the light of their criticism.

Members of our faculty often get together evenings for social affairs. We really enjoy each other socially.[9]

[8]*Ibid.*, p. 165.
[9]*Ibid.*, p. 167.

Those teachers judged unfavorable toward curriculum improvement made these statements about relationships with fellow teachers:

I don't appreciate criticism from other teachers, for they don't know my problem.

Small group work is a waste of time except within departments.

We need more chances for social life together. This might help build better morale among staff members.

There is too much partiality shown to the older teachers in our school.

We don't discuss new methods with each other. One just goes ahead on his own, for each teacher has the right to do what he thinks best in his own classes.

I miss the fellowship with other faculty members in a social way. We never do anything together outside of school.

I hesitate to use new methods because the older teachers often resent any change in ways of working with pupils.

There is definite favoritism on our faculty. Some teachers get extra pay for showy performances like band and dramatics.

In working with others in curriculum improvement, I would want them to be open-minded, creative, lack prejudice, and have interests outside their own department.

New ideas are not welcomed here. One receives little or no support from others in attempting to change the curriculum.[10]

The area of teacher-parent relationships presents the greatest number of barriers in the views of the teachers in this sample. In fact, *only one* group of teachers felt that parent relationships were nearly what they should be. Here is what they said:

The goals and practices of teachers and parents, in our school, seem to be quite similar.

In our school, 50–75 per cent of the parents try to implement good study habits with our pupils.

[10]*Ibid.*, p. 169.

Criticism from a certain group of our parents helps me re-evaluate my class work.

A carefully selected group of parents might be very helpful in planning curriculum-improvement programs.

As parents and teachers work together we get to know each other better, and teachers also get a better understanding of their pupils.

A small portion of our parents appear to be interested in curriculum-improvement programs in our school. They are the parents of superior pupils and have an above average educational background.[11]

Since almost all of the teachers in this sample felt parent-teacher relationships were shaky and nonsupportive of curriculum-improvement programs, comments were plentiful and decidedly negative in tone:

Parents don't seem to be concerned enough to support P. T. A. or other school organizations.

There is practically no similarity between the goals of parents and teachers.

Parental criticism is of no value to me, since they never criticize unless they want to fuss about low grades.

We get no support from our parents for curriculum-improvement programs. Their only interest seems to be in the pupil just passing the class work.

Our parents don't know enough to criticize our teaching methods.

Parents in our school support athletics, not the academic program.

Apathy and ignorance are to blame for lack of interest in the school by the parents.

Parents are interested only in grades, not in curriculum-improvement programs. They are not capable of curriculum planning with teachers.

[11]*Ibid.*, pp. 172–173.

Our parents have little or no contact with the schools. They seem completely unconcerned.

We have so little personal contact with parents that it is impossible to get a good picture of the pupils' home background.

Parents do not support the school program; yet they always telephone to complain about poor grades.

Our teachers and parents never get together in a social way.

Most of our parents are textile workers, so the standards of teachers and parents are too different for them to be able to work together in curriculum planning.

The apathetic attitude of parents toward the school is reflected in the pupils.

We have very poor communication with parents, as they do not attend school functions or come to have conferences with the teachers.

We do not know what goals the parents hold for their children, as they never come to discuss this with us.

Our curriculum-improvement programs are much better off without parents around.

The parents we need to see never come to school.

Parents can't help plan the curriculum, for they have no idea of what it should contain.[12]

In the area of teacher-pupil relationships, the teachers who were judged favorable to curriculum improvement commented as follows:

We have good teacher-pupil relationships in my classes, as evidenced by the spontaneity of the pupils in their class work.

Pupil planning is very important to me and the pupils. It brings about greater pupil interest, satisfaction, and participation.

Our teachers enjoy working in co-curricular activities, as it seems to enhance teacher-pupil relationships.

[12]*Ibid.*, pp. 174–175.

Dealing with individual differences is very realistic, yet very difficult to accomplish in mixed ability groupings.

Teaching my pupils is a mutual growth experience, for I can see changes in me and in their behavior patterns as the school year moves onward.

Pupils are not harder to teach today than in past years, for pupils come to school today with more knowledge and a readiness to grasp new ideas more freely.[13]

Those teachers who were judged unfavorable in the teacher-pupil area made the following statements:

Yes, it is important for pupils to share planning and evaluation procedures; but the process is too unwieldy for me to use in my classes.

I cannot handle individual differences adequately. The time is too short and the pupils too many.

It is completely unimportant for teachers to sponsor co-curricular activities.

Pupils are much harder to teach today than formerly, because of restlessness, excessive demands, poor home conditions, and lack of desire for academic success.

Pupil planning is fine with bright pupils, but very poor with slow groups.

Dealing with individual differences is not very realistic in an average class, since one real problem can throw the entire class.

My pupils are so restless and tense most of the time that I find it difficult to see any changed behavior patterns on their part.

The pupils we teach have no interest in sharing the responsibility for class planning. They prefer to leave it all for me to do.

Most of my pupils seem to lack interest in school. They have too many outside interests competing for their time and attention.

My pupils do not have enough responsibility given to them by parents to help them develop a sound sense of values.

[13]*Ibid.*, pp. 178–179.

Pupils I teach today do not try as hard or work as hard as they once did.

Many of our pupils have a defiant attitude toward learning, and this attitude makes it impossible to achieve good relationships with them in the classroom.[14]

It is apparent that teachers do feel keenly about the way other persons work with them and that warm supportive relationships tend to eliminate barriers while nonsupportive or antagonistic relationships tend to erect them. Considerably more research is needed in this area of personal and professional relationships of teachers and those who work closely with them in educating youth. Hopefully, added insights will reduce the number of barriers to curriculum improvement.

SUGGESTED READINGS

Association for Supervision and Curriculum Development. *Action For Curriculum Improvement*. Washington: The Association, 1951.
———. *Research For Curriculum Improvement*. Washington: The Association, 1957.
Banning, Evelyn I. "Teacher Attitudes Toward Curriculum Change, A Study of the Junior High School Teachers of Pittsfield." Unpublished doctoral dissertation, Harvard, 1951.
Cay, Donald F. "Selected Teachers' Expressed Judgments Concerning Barriers to Curriculum Improvement." Unpublished doctoral dissertation, University of Florida, 1960.
Doll, Ronald C. *Curriculum Improvement: Decision-Making and Process*. Boston: Allyn and Bacon, Inc., 1964.
Douglas, Harl R., ed. *The High School Curriculum*. New York: Ronald Press, 1964.
Duncan, James K. "An Instrument for Measuring Readiness for Curriculum Change." Unpublished doctoral dissertation, University of Florida, 1954.
Fullagar, William A. "Some Teacher Sensed Problems in Curriculum Improvement." Unpublished doctoral dissertation, Columbia University, 1951.
Sharp, George. *Curriculum Development as Re-education of the Teacher*. New York: Teachers College, Columbia University, 1951.

[14]*Ibid.*, pp. 181–182.

Shuster, Albert H., and Ploghoft, Milton E. *The Emerging Elementary Curriculum*. Columbus, Ohio: Charles E. Merrill Books, Inc., 1963.

Simons, B. L. "Obstacles to Curriculum Development," *National Association of Secondary School Principals Bulletin*, 43 (February 1959) 26–29.

Taba, Hilda. *Curriculum Development—Theory and Practice*. New York: Harcourt, Brace and World, Inc., 1962.

Wiles, Kimball. *The Changing Curriculum of the American High School*. Englewood Cliffs, N. J.: Prentice-Hall, Inc., 1963.

X

CURRENT PLANS AND PRACTICES IN CURRICULUM ORGANIZATION

As one looks at the development of curriculum in American public schools, it is apparent that, as the needs of society changed, curriculum changed. There has always been, however, a considerable lag between social change and curriculum change. Throughout history, people have tended to look on innovation with suspicion. Anything that was different from the accepted way of doing things was sure to arouse some objectors to a frenzy of talk and action, thus slowing down the process of change. Today the time has arrived when the changes in education must be hastened if curriculums are to deal successfully with the realities of our generation and of those to come.

CURRENT PLANS OF ORGANIZATION

In looking over American public schools for curricular organization, one finds very few types of organization that are very different from traditional patterns. Here and there a new plan exists, but for the most part curriculums are still organized in the traditional manner.

On the elementary-school level, the major departure from tradition is the ungraded plan, which removes traditional grade barriers and allows pupils to move at their own pace. In the secondary schools, one finds some implementation of the Trump Plan, which organizes teachers and pupils by a plan of large-group instruction, small-group instruction, and independent study time. This plan, which represents quite a departure from the traditional time-organization plans of most secondary schools, makes great use of audio-visual aids, team teaching, and teacher aides. Another new idea is the "phase learning" concept of secondary education, which is being used at Melbourne High School, near Cape Kennedy, Florida. This plan for secondary schools departs as much from the traditional as the ungraded primary plan does for elementary schools and is, in reality, an ungraded high school.

In addition to the plans described, there are new techniques (such as teaching by television), programmed learning with machines and textbooks, and various methods of grouping pupils to narrow the range of abilities in any one class. Although all these are peripheral to major curriculum change, they are necessary to encourage new approaches. Every small segment of experimentation with new media for teaching may help to build the foundation for better curriculum.

According to Taba,[1] current curriculum practices can be divided into five general plans: (1) subject organization, (2) broad-fields curriculum, (3) curriculum based on social processes and life functions, (4) the activity or experience curriculum, and (5) the core curriculum. Under one or more of these headings would fall the terms, such as *fusion, correlation, integration,* and *unit developments,* that are used to designate combinations of subject matter.

Of the five plans, the traditional subject-matter organization is far and away the most commonly used. From the earliest teaching and learning situations came this simple organization. Because it is easy to administer and easy to allot credits to single-subject courses, this plan has remained as the predominant pattern of organization, despite some strong criticism of it.

Some of this criticism stems from the fact that this type of organization tends to compartmentalize learning and often has little positive value for the growing pupil. It also tends to revere the past and to overlook the developments of the present, placing a premium

[1]Hilda Taba, *Curriculum Development: Theory and Practice* (New York: Harcourt, Brace and World, Inc., 1962), pp. 382–412.

upon rote memorization rather than on the ability to solve problems. Because much criticism was aimed at the limited number of subjects offered, many schools have added numerous new subjects to this curriculum, but the basic pattern remains. Recently this pattern has received additional support as college subject-matter specialists have experimented with placing more advanced subject matter at a much lower grade level in the public schools.

Taba offers the following caution with respect to this movement:

Currently there is again an emphasis on content, disciplined knowledge, and the lifting of the intellectual level by a return to compartmentalized subjects, even in the elementary schools. It is only to be hoped that at least some of the weaknesses noted in the earlier type of subject organization will not be repeated, and that the new emphasis on content will be implemented by a clearer understanding of the ways in which disciplined knowledge can be brought closer to the minds of children and youth.[2]

Many of our secondary schools use the broad-fields approach to curriculum organization. This pattern, developed as a possible answer to criticisms of the subject-matter organization, attempts to reduce the separateness of subjects and to blend related areas together. Here, areas of study come under headings such as natural sciences, the social sciences, the language arts, and the physical sciences, and an attempt is made to bring into any one of these areas common principles that can cut across the subject-matter divisions. As an example, one finds courses taught under titles such as "Literature and American History," "Biology and Human Life," "The Geography of History," and "Social Problems." One danger of this organization is a tendency toward large generalizations. However, the broad-fields type of organization does provide a more functional approach to learning, and the relatedness of its content should be more significant to learners than the separated content of some other methods.

Some schools have tried a curriculum pattern organized around the social processes or life functions of man, with emphasis upon

[2]*Ibid.*, pp. 392–393.

the close relationship between its content and life. Its proponents point out that, with such a central focus, the curriculum will bring about a needed integration of knowledge and a clearer connection between knowledge and students' daily living. Units of study are centered around subjects such as health, responsibilities of citizenship, personal relationships with others, economics, religion, and aesthetics. Although the plan stresses the unification of learning under the persistent life functions common to man, it draws heavily upon traditional subject-matter content to attempt to accomplish these aims. Because the organization of content under this plan is so different from traditional organization, and the methods and techniques recommended are also different from traditional ones, it has suffered from a lack of teachers trained to implement it.

Another type of curriculum pattern is called the activity or the experience curriculum. This type of organization is built upon the concept that learning and the interests and needs of the students should be joined and upon the belief that the learner must be involved in present problems in order for learning to have meaning. Based on the growth and developmental patterns of children, this plan uses the principles of human growth and development and their sequential patterns to identify centers of interest. The terms "persistent life situations" and "present life situations" are often used to describe the subject-matter organization of this curriculum, which has been used mainly at the elementary level, including the sixth grade. Hopkins describes the content of such a curriculum as follows:

> Since the emphasis is upon improvement of growth in individual learners in and through group contacts, a curriculum becomes a series of experiences in which all individuals improve the process of achieving more intelligent human relationships. It is present living made into better present living for everyone concerned through cooperative interaction.[3]

A plan of curricular organization that has been used experimen-

[3]L. T. Hopkins, *Interaction: The Democratic Process* (Boston: D. C. Heath and Co., 1941), p. 39.

tally in many junior high and high schools is the core curriculum. Core programs generally are characterized by extended periods of time and by a fusion or interrelatedness of subject matter from more than one area of knowledge. Usually the programs are unified attempts to search out answers to big problems by drawing upon the subject matter of several areas of knowledge. The core of learning may be organized around problems and needs of adolescents or it may be centered around problems of living. One of the main characteristics of a true core program is its goal of focusing the study around student interests and real problems of living. It is definitely pupil-oriented in its outlook and operation.

NEW CONTENT WITHIN SUBJECT AREAS

As was pointed out earlier, a great deal of effort has been directed toward including new content in particular subject-matter areas of the curriculum. For the past ten years, scientists, mathematicians, and foreign-language specialists in particular have done much to put new content into their areas of the curriculum. Progress of this nature does not reflect curriculum building, but rather a kind of reworking and renovation of existing curriculums. Rather than making any basic change in the design of curriculum, this approach merely tailors the content to modern knowledge. Often private foundations or the government has financed studies in the areas mentioned; such studies have most certainly stimulated new thought and interest in what to teach and when to teach it. Although many of these study groups have confined their efforts to the high school, some of them have projected a sequence all through the elementary school and high school.

The results of these specific studies within certain disciplines have been, for the most part, stimulating to all the other areas. New methods of teaching and new procedural techniques have developed as a part of these studies, and these are helpful by-products of the work. Although one could not describe this kind of study as major curriculum building, it does represent a healthy search for better practices and content within certain disciplines. There is hope in the fact that studies are also being authorized and financed in disciplines other than those of a scientific or mathematical nature. Such work is badly needed in the humanities and social sciences, for they also contribute greatly to the educated man in America.

WHAT PROGRESS HAS BEEN MADE?

Back in the 1930's, great emphasis was placed upon the learner and his social and psychological development as a basis for new curriculums. Today the air is filled with demands to emphasize the academic disciplines and to minimize the social development of the pupil. The great argument of the 1930's goes on again today, but the other side of the coin is up. When one examines curriculum logically, it becomes apparent that both subject matter and the nature of the learner must be carefully considered; one without the other makes an inadequate approach to curriculum. Fortunately today's movement toward content promotes *principles of learning*, discovery, and inquiry, along with additional content mastery. This is an approach far different from rote memorization of content just for the sake of mastery of more information. Now the emphasis is upon using the content as a background for further inquiry and intellectual growth.

Certainly there has been some progress in curriculum building in the past thirty years. School buildings and facilities have been tremendously improved and enriched. Materials of instruction have been greatly diversified. Today's pupil has more learning aids at his disposal than any pupil at any other time in history. He gets numerous opportunities to learn by seeing, which helps believing. The school of today and its curriculum are geared to stimulate intellectual excitement for pupils and teachers. School has become an interesting place, as the pupils are offered diversified approaches to learning.

But where do we go from here? An excellent example of the kinds of questions that need to be asked concerning curriculum building for the 1960's and future decades is given in an article by Fraser and Pullen:

1. Who should make curriculum decisions?
2. How can schools effectively use the recommendations from nationally oriented curriculum projects in specific subject fields?
3. How can the curriculum be developed to meet the needs of all members of the school population?
4. What should be included and excluded in planning the school curriculum?
5. What priorities and balance should be established in the instructional program?
6. To what extent should the content, structure, and organization of the academic disciplines determine the content and nature of the academic subjects in the instructional program in the schools?[4]

In a summary at the end of the article, the authors emphasize the importance of cooperative efforts:

As these and related issues concerning what to teach are considered, there are several groups that should participate in the process. They include classroom teachers, school administrators, academic scholars, scholars in professional education, and informed lay persons. Each has a special contribution to make, and each must respect and utilize the contributions of the others. Only through such cooperative efforts can our schools provide instructional programs that will meet the demands of the 1960's—and the decades to come.[5]

A large part of the dissension in curriculum building of the past has resulted from the tendency of the various levels of schooling to become self-enclosed entities. The elementary school, the secondary school, and the college or university became separate institutions with little or no interest in the level above or below. Each of these levels congratulated itself on its strengths and blamed all of its failures on the level below; however, they seldom did any real investigation of the work going on at another level. Far too rarely do

[4]Dorothy M. Fraser and Thomas G. Pullen, Jr., "What To Teach?" *National Education Association Journal*, 51 (October 1962), pp. 34–36.
[5]*Ibid*., p. 36.

we find elementary, junior high, high school, and college teachers sitting down together to work out their common problems.

An outstanding example of the kind of necessary cooperative effort for improved curriculum has already been mentioned. In the city of Toronto, a close working relationship has been established between the Board of Education and the University of Toronto. This relationship was formally established in 1960 through the formation of a Joint University-Board Committee whose major function was to study the question of whether or not secondary school teaching reflected contemporary conceptions of the subjects being taught. As a result of the committee's study, a negative answer was found to the question.[6] Elementary, high school, and university teachers on this committee then began working together at rebuilding the curriculum.

THE NEED FOR CURRICULUM THEORY

There has been a great deal of discussion of the need for theory in curriculum building, but as yet there is no identifiable field of curriculum theory. Many curriculums are resting upon learning theory or human growth and development theory, but not a clear-cut curriculum theory.

To expect to devise a purely scientific theory for curriculum is probably unrealistic. Pupils and teachers are human, and a part of being human seems to be to resist scientific analysis. How far can one go in predicting how a certain pattern of curriculum will produce preconceived results with a special group of pupils? In the final analysis, no curriculum can be more than a broad outline until teachers and pupils begin to work together in the classroom.

It is not intended to imply that we need *a* theory—a sort of master theory to guide all curriculum construction. Considering differences among various types of communities in the United States and the differences among school districts, no one theory could fulfill the needs of all schools. Rather, we need several different theories, all of which have some common factors but also the ability to pro-

[6]Frye, *Design for Learning*, p. 3.

duce slightly different products. One theory would be highly undesirable and would certainly lead to mass conformity, a state not suited to the American taste. Many theories would lead to a sense of rivalry and competition, and this *is* in keeping with the American value system. The theories may well be a combination of science and artistic expression, for teaching is a combination of science and art. One without the other leaves much to be desired; the combination is what produces a master teacher. The theory builders will need both the imagination of the creative artist and the objectivity of the scientist to build effective, useful curriculum theories.

THE TRUMP PLAN AND OTHER INNOVATIONS

In many sections of the country, secondary schools are experimenting with the Trump Plan (page 154) for more effective utilization of time and staff. Team teaching is at the heart of the concept, along with large-group instruction, small-group instruction, and independent study time for pupils. In broad outline, it is recommended that 40 per cent of the pupils' time be scheduled in large groups, 30 per cent in seminars or small groups, and 30 per cent in individual study. Physical facilities of the school building must be adapted to such a schedule. Large rooms are needed for groups of 125-135 pupils so that the teaching teams may use all types of audio-visual aids to present their material, while seminar rooms should be available for small groups of 12-16 pupils. Study booths and carrels, with recording and listening equipment, are needed for individual study.

In the large groups, teaching teams present basic information to all pupils taking the course. Then, in small groups, pupils and teachers explore concepts at a deeper level. In the individual study time, the pupil, with teacher consultation whenever necessary, goes into real depth in areas that are geared to his own ability and interest. For instance, a pupil who is deeply interested in science may follow an experiment to a level comparable to college work.

During all phases of the program, the pupil is constantly encouraged to take increasing amounts of responsibility for his own learning. Since the number of pupils in a seminar is limited to 12–16, each member has a turn as student chairman, and this brings increased involvement. In such a small group each student feels responsible for the smooth operation of the group, and this brings responsibility for preparation and participation. With this background of participation in the small group, the pupil builds confidence to embark on projects in his individual study time. Emphasis on the individual's responsibility for his own learning is bound to increase in future curriculum building.

Some schools are experimenting with only part of the Trump Plan. Most often they are trying team teaching, one of whose major benefits is the crossing of subject-matter lines and the reduction of compartmentalized knowledge.

Numerous other new patterns of content organization and presentation are also being tried. In many secondary schools, one finds a combination work-study plan designed for young people who will terminate their formal education with high-school graduation. Many of these students need to earn money to complete high school. Under this plan, pupils spend half the day in school studying basic skill subjects and the other half working in factories, business houses, and professional offices in the community. The major responsibility for such a program belongs to the vocational teacher, who is responsible for follow-up as well as for job placement. Enrollment in these programs is usually limited to high-school juniors and seniors. Work-study programs do not claim to be a panacea; however, they help to hold young people in school until graduation. Although these programs are only a partial answer to reducing the number of high-school drop-outs, they deserve further experimentation.

In cooperation with the College Entrance Board, many high schools have joined the Advanced Placement Program. Under this plan, which was designed to assist superior college-bound students, the student who passes a required examination and has the recommendation of his high school can do college-level work and receive college credit under the direction of qualified high-school teachers.

For every college credit earned in high school, the student receives advanced standing upon college entrance. He bypasses certain required courses and moves directly into more advanced work.

Another attempt to break away from the tight compartmentalization of knowledge of the traditionally organized high school is block-of-time scheduling, which has been most frequently used at the junior high level in modified core programs. By extending the length of time spent by pupils with one teacher, it is felt that both pupils and teachers can know each other better and work together better. In a survey of block-of-time scheduling practices in Illinois junior high schools, it was found that 61 per cent of the schools sampled were using such a method of scheduling.[7] The participants made the following statements in favor of block-of-time scheduling:

1. A pupil can know well one teacher and a teacher can easily learn more about a given pupil. Thus, pupils tend to feel wanted and perhaps more secure.
2. The learning situation profits from increased laboratory work, more effective field trips, better use of audio-visual materials, and enhanced opportunities to practice desired skills and to develop appropriate attitudes and appreciations.
3. Learners are more inclined to acquire knowledge of self as well as skills in group processes and human relations.
4. Improvement in thinking skills is more likely to occur as the concept of pupil-teacher planning is explored and implemented.
5. Fruitful guidance opportunities multiply and pupils more readily work toward a philosophy of life.
6. Concepts of democratic living come alive as they broaden and become more deeply imbedded in the minds of pupils.
7. Integration of learning experiences is enhanced as subject barriers fade away and language arts and reading, for example, in part become important to *all* teachers.[8]

All of these claims for block-of-time practices represent some of the

[7]Illinois Superintendent of Public Instruction, *Block-Of-Time Scheduling Practices in Illinois Junior High Schools*, (Springfield: State of Illinois, 1960). [8]*Ibid.*, p. 35.

goals for which educators have been striving for half a century.

An added feature of recent curriculum organizational patterns has been an extensive amount of experimentation with grouping of pupils by such criteria as intelligence, achievement, age level, interest, and ability. Group size has also been experimented with; some classes have been greatly enlarged while others have been substantially reduced. For teaching certain basic skills, group size can often be increased, but for depth exploration of content, it is obvious that a small group is necessary for student-teacher interaction and discussion.

It would probably be safe to say that more curriculum change has taken place in the secondary school since Sputnik than in the previous thirty-year period. In spite of the fact that the five basic curriculum patterns have not changed appreciably, the component parts of secondary schooling have begun to be modernized and to have greater utility for today's youth. At long last, the secondary school is moving in a constructive way to improve its curriculums.

SUGGESTED READINGS

Beauchamp, George A. *Curriculum Theory*. Willmette, Illinois: The Kagg Press, 1961.

Brown, B. Frank. "The Non-Graded High School," *Phi Delta Kappan*, XLIV (February 1963).

Douglas, Harl. *Education for Life Adjustment: Its Meaning and Implementation*. New York: Ronald Press, 1950.

Faunce, R. C., and Bossing, N. R. *Developing the Core Curriculum*. 2nd ed. Englewood Cliffs, N. J.: Prentice-Hall, Inc., 1958.

Frye, Northrop, ed. *Design for Learning*. Toronto: University of Toronto Press, 1962.

Goodlad, John I., and Anderson, Robert. *The Nongraded Elementary School*. New York: Harcourt, Brace and Co., Inc., 1959.

Haan, Aubrey. *Elementary School Curriculum: Theory and Research*. Boston: Allyn and Bacon, Inc., 1961.

Herrick, Virgil E., and Tyler, Ralph W. eds. *Toward Improved Curriculum Theory*. Supplementary Educational Monograph No. 71. Chicago: University of Chicago Press, 1950.

Hopkins, L. T. *Interaction: The Democratic Process*. Boston: D. C. Heath Co., 1941.

Illinois Superintendent of Public Instruction. *Block-of-Time Scheduling Practices in Illinois Junior High Schools.* Springfield: State of Illinois, 1960.

Saylor, J. G., and Alexander, W. M. *Curriculum Planning for Better Teaching and Learning.* New York: Rinehart & Co., 1954.

Taba, Hilda. *Curriculum Development: Theory and Practice.* New York: Harcourt, Brace & World, Inc., 1962.

Wiles, Kimball. *The Changing Curriculum of the American High School.* Englewood Cliffs, N. J.: Prentice-Hall, Inc., 1963.

XI

IMMEDIATE TASKS FOR BETTER CURRICULUMS

Within the framework of public education as it is now organized lie many points of attack for better curriculums. To be sure, there are many realistic limitations within which school systems must work. Many systems do not have the available time, money, or materials to do the kind of curriculum improvement program they would like to do, whereas others have teachers with less than top-quality preparation and training. Regardless of the limitations, in any school system there are some things that can be done to improve curriculum.

Perhaps the first important step that any system can take is recognizing the need for improvement. Willingness to admit that times have changed and that one is ready to re-examine what is being taught and measure its current effectiveness will open the way for progress. As soon as one faces the fact that curriculum can be improved, he has made the first step in doing something about it. Whether the next step be large or small does not make too much difference. That the step *is* taken makes all the difference between a live, vibrant school or a dead, rigid, inflexible one. Flexibility is the keynote to progress in public education, just as it is in life itself. Unfortunately, rigidity sets in very quickly in institutions, and educators must be ever watchful to maintain a high degree of resiliency in the curriculum.

WHERE TO START

For thirty or more years now, the schools have been adding new courses at a very rapid rate, but dropping hardly any; curriculum change has been mostly an additive process. At the start of any program of improvement, each item in the curriculum should be examined to see if it should be continued or if it is no longer necessary. The existing curriculum should be studied on both a vertical and horizontal level. The horizontal study will give data on the scope and sequence of a specific subject-matter area within a grade level and will provide many opportunities for all teachers of the same grade level or discipline to work together and minutely examine their offerings. On the other hand, the vertical study examines a given area from the first grade through the twelfth and brings together teachers from all different levels of the school system and various depths of subject matter.

Too much of the curriculum-improvement work of the past has been a hodgepodge effort without careful determination of goals and objectives. At the start of any new program, take a long look at existing goals and objectives and see if they really meet the needs of today's pupils. Decide in an orderly fashion which goals are still valid and which ones need to be discarded or replaced by more realistic ones.

Immediate consideration should also be given to the ways in which children learn. How much does a child learn when the teacher does most of the thinking for him? How much of the learning responsibility belongs to the teaching staff and how much belongs to the pupil? Until such decisions are made, schools will go on in the same old way.

Certainly, at the start of any curriculum-improvement program professional materials, such as curriculum guides and bulletins, should be readily available to all teachers.

School systems that have not already done so need to establish professional libraries and instructional materials centers for teachers. The mere fact that such a professional resource center is available encourages teachers to improve themselves and their teaching practices.

One of the pressing needs of schools, in order to build better curriculums, lies in the school buildings and physical facilities. Improved buildings can help establish an atmosphere which is conducive to stimulating classroom learning. Warm, complementary colors used on classroom walls tend to make a comfortable working situation and are pleasing to the aesthetic sense. Flexibility in classroom design and movable furniture make it possible to adjust the room to the specific activity underway at a particular time. There are times when students will meet as a total group and other times when they will be divided into four or five small groups.

Comfortable, attractive recreation areas for pupils will help to make the student body feel at home and able to enjoy the sociability of their peers. It will also help to reduce hall congestion during the lunch hours and keep pupils constructively occupied in free time.

Many recently constructed school buildings show evidence of one or all of these features. Nevertheless, there are still too many outmoded buildings being used that lack any of these desirable features. For instance, the library in the modern school has browsing areas for pupils and a lounging area where they can read in comfortable chairs and sofas. It may also be equipped with many electronic devices that permit listening and recording by pupils. It is no longer the tomblike facility of yesteryear. What we need are modern buildings that contain these desirable features. All youngsters deserve the chance to enjoy fine buildings and modern facilities.

DECISIONS REGARDING FUNCTION

Many lay citizens and educators have criticized the school for assuming some of the functions that traditionally belonged to the home, the church, and other social agencies of the community. The charge has been made that the public school is trying to become entirely too broad in the tasks it undertakes, and this charge is not without substance. Responsibility for social and emotional development, it has been suggested, is not the primary business of the school.

The school should, the critics say, concern itself with intellectual growth and development, for this is the proper function of education.

Although one must admit that intellectual growth is the major function of schools, it becomes increasingly difficult to justify this as the only function. Social and emotional problems, as has been widely proved by research, act as blocks to learning. When a youngster has such problems, the realistic teacher knows that assistance must be given before effective learning can be expected.

One of the areas in which the school has assumed a great degree of responsibility in the past thirty years is that of social growth. Undoubtedly, the school has some measure of legitimate interest in this area of the child's growth. The question involves the degree of interest. Many schools have overdone their concern with social growth to the detriment of the intellectual aspect of the educational program. There is need for a rethinking and redefinition by the school of how much responsibility it should take for a pupil's social development. Whether the pupils come from homes and neighborhoods that are socially and culturally disadvantaged will have much to do with the final decision as to what emphasis this phase of curriculum is given. In many of the larger urban areas, pupils in schools five miles apart come from different worlds. Pupils from the disadvantaged areas might never have the chance to learn proper manners if it were not for the school. On the other hand, for the children from culturally advantaged homes time spent on these same items is a waste of school time. In describing human-relations education, in the Wilmington, Delaware, school system, Crosby explains curriculum building with disadvantaged children:

It was essential that the teachers develop a clear understanding of the values and goals underlying the human-relations curriculum. In the past, teachers had frequently been concerned with developing a curriculum that would be effective in relaying information to children. Here the goal in curriculum planning is to help children deal with their problems in home and community life. This means that merely imparting information will be ineffective. The children must be taught to build concepts and apply generalizations. Thus, a knowledge of the learning process in the light of the peculiar needs of disadvantaged children becomes an essential prerequisite to effective teaching.

This approach to curriculum required that the teacher develop a completely new set of skills. The skills of curriculum planning are intricate, and the development of a new program calls for a thorough re-evaluation of existing methods. In addition, these teachers had to learn to use a wide variety of sociometric instruments and to apply the information obtained as a basis for their curriculum design. Freedom to build curriculum appropriate to the learners, without following set patterns in guides and textbooks, requires not only skill, but an inner security which frees the teacher to experiment, to take failure in stride, and to develop uniqueness in teaching.[1]

The example given above is based upon careful examination of the home backgrounds of the pupils and upon much sociometric information. These pupils needed the human-relations education curriculum with heavy emphasis upon social growth. For the disadvantaged youth, this type of curriculum offered the most feasible method of serving their needs. Based upon need such as this and data that substantiates the need, the curriculum design is well founded. Most public-school systems should make such surveys and ascertain the most vital areas of need for their particular pupils.

USING OUTSIDE CURRICULUM STUDIES

One of the shaping forces of curriculum in the sixties has been the national studies in certain academic disciplines (pages 93-94). Although the new programs that have grown out of these studies may be helpful, teachers need to question the purpose and scope of the studies. Some of these new programs have been tested only on youngsters of high achievement. They have been designed only for the college bound and really do not have any place with average or slow pupils in high school. Instead of adopting all the new ideas, wholesale, teachers and administrators need to look into the background of

[1]Muriel Crosby, "Curriculum Implications of Human Relations Education," *Theory Into Practice*, I (October 1962), 196.

each study carefully. After thorough checking, they may find that a particular study is not appropriate for their school and should be rejected. On the other hand, there may be some parts that can be easily adapted for certain pupils.

Often curriculum studies by individual school systems have much to offer. However, a comparison of schools and pupils is necessary in order to ascertain whether or not the experimental program will serve well in one's own school system. Unfortunately many school persons have tended to become "band-wagon riders" in regard to new curriculum proposals. Whether the new program was applicable or not to their local systems, they have instituted it quickly, only to see it shortly fall apart and disappear.

ARTICULATION

One of the weakest parts of most system's curriculum lies in the area of articulation of program. As we have seen (Chapter VIII) the term *articulation* is a professional one that designates coordination, continuity, and unification of learning experiences from one grade level to another throughout the entire school experience. There is little doubt that pupils do face unnecessary problems as they move from one level of school to the next. Secondary-school teachers, for example, often have little or no idea of what the pupils are taught at the level of the elementary school. Since they do not know much about what has preceded the pupils' entrance into the secondary school, they often proceed on false assumptions about the pupils' backgrounds. Such procedure may embitter the pupils early in their secondary-school career and prejudice them against high school. Of immediate concern to school systems is how to reduce the number of such problems, caused by lack of continuity and poor articulation of learning experiences.

One approach is through an in-service curriculum-building project. Teachers who make up the curriculum committees that work on a vertical study of the learning experiences are in the best position to discover the cause of the difficulty. When elementary and secondary teachers begin to work together in a group, they usually begin to see each other's point of view. As they begin to see what is important to the other teachers, they also begin to see gaps in the curriculum and begin to devise ways to close these gaps and improve the continuity.

For a truly effective program of articulation to take place, it is necessary for teachers to work together closely on a regular basis, planning and evaluating the entire curriculum together.

One portion of the problem of inarticulation may be alleviated, as the Association for Supervision and Curriculum Development points out in their 1958 yearbook, by colleges in their teacher education programs:

> Further, many inarticulations in schools seem to result from a lack of understanding on the part of teachers at one level of what teachers at another level are seeking to accomplish. This situation gives rise to some questions which teacher education institutions should answer: How much of the essential professional curriculum for elementary-school teachers should be different from that for secondary-school teachers? Wherein should teachers of different school levels be similarly educated? When the curriculum for one group of teachers is different from that of another group, why is it different? When curricula are the same, why are they the same? How much provision is made to teach prospective elementary-school teachers to understand the secondary school to which their prospective pupils will go? How much effort is made to teach secondary-school teachers to understand the program of the elementary schools from which their prospective pupils come?[2]

Although some attempts have been made at articulation on the high-school level for the academically talented pupils as they move toward college, little has been done for the pupil who will move into the work world. Much could be done between school and community to narrow the gap between high-school graduation and entrance into the economic life of the community. The school has just as great an obligation to those pupils who terminate their formal edu-

[2]Association for Supervision and Curriculum Development, *A Look at Continuity in the School Program* (Washington: The Association, 1958), p. 269.

cation at the end of high school as it does to those who go on to higher education. In recent years, public-school curriculums have stressed work for the slow learner and the academically talented; yet they have done little to enrich the curriculum for the average pupil who makes up the bulk of high-school populations. In the future, increased emphasis needs to be directed to this type of pupil.

NEED FOR GUIDANCE SERVICES

Guidance counselors should be available from the elementary school level on up through the secondary school and college levels. Most secondary schools have done well in obtaining as adequate a staff as the budget will allow for guidance services. The junior high schools are trying to offer this service as often as they can. A few elementary schools have also added this service, but many more need to do so. If guidance personnel can work with the elementary-school child, certain corrective measures may be started early enough in the child's school life to offer him some real assistance.

In many schools the ratio of counselors to pupils should be reduced, because an overloaded counselor can actually do little for pupils beyond administering the standardized testing program—and the job of vocational testing and counseling is growing larger as each year passes. An adequate guidance staff helps to satisfy the immediate needs of public schools in order to build better curriculums. The guidance personnel are often the only ones who can bring a resolution to problems that plague the pupils, administrators, and teachers.

NEED FOR IMPROVED PUBLIC RELATIONS

Public school systems embarking upon programs of curriculum building must remember that parents and other school patrons like to be informed concerning potential changes in curriculum. If they are well informed prior to the time changes are made, members of the community are usually supportive of the school and its program. As discussed in Chapter V, lay advisory councils composed of local citizens who have demonstrated interest in school problems often serve as the best communication line to the community. The school should also use all available communications media such as newspaper, radio, and television to keep the public informed. By improving its public-relations program, a school puts itself in a most advantageous position to obtain support for curriculum improvement.

NEED TO ENCOURAGE RESEARCH

If a school system wishes to change curriculum, it needs to encourage research projects among the staff. A school system that encourages research and experimentation among its teachers is always growing. As a safeguard, before importing wholesale a change that has proved valuable in another system, it is wise to try it out in a pilot project. From the evaluation of pilot projects comes the substantiating data that may encourage widespread use of a new technique or new content. Another safeguard is a community survey to sample opinion regarding projected changes. Research projects and pilot studies or surveys help to bring about change in an orderly, evolutionary way. Change accomplished in this way is usually of longer duration and has a greater degree of acceptability than does revolutionary progress.

In spite of the limitations of time, money, and materials in many school systems, there is opportunity for all to experiment and grow. A large portion of successful curriculum improvement lies in the state of mind with which a school system approaches it, and an open mind and a willingness to experiment can do much to overcome limitations. Enthusiastic patrons, teachers, pupils, and administrators have accomplished feats that others might have considered impossible. To begin to work is the way to success in curriculum building.

SUGGESTED READINGS

Andrew, Dean C., and Willey, Roy D. *Administration and Organization of the Guidance Program*. New York: Harper & Brothers, 1958.

Association for Supervision and Curriculum Development. *A Look at Continuity in the School Program.* Washington: The Association, 1958.

———. *Leadership in Improving Instruction.* Washington: The Association, 1960.

Caswell, Hollis L., *et al. Curriculum Improvement in Public School Systems.* New York: Bureau of Publications, Teachers College, Columbia University, 1950.

Crosby, Muriel. "Curriculum Implications of Human Relations Education," *Theory Into Practice,* I (October 1962), pp. 191–196.

Dahlke, H. Otto. *Values in Culture and Classroom: A Study in the Sociology of the School.* New York: Harper & Brothers, 1958.

"Disaffected Children and Youth," *Educational Leadership,* 20, (February 1963).

Doll, Ronald C. *Curriculum Improvement: Decision-Making and Process.* Boston: Allyn and Bacon, Inc., 1964.

Doll, Ronald C., *et al. Organizing for Curriculum Improvement.* New York: Bureau of Publications, Teachers College, Columbia University, 1953.

Kelley, Earl. *The Workshop Way of Learning.* New York: Harper & Brothers, 1951.

Krug, E. A. *Curriculum Planning.* New York: Harper & Brothers, 1950.

Krug, E. A., *et al. Administering Curriculum Planning.* New York: Harper & Brothers, 1956.

McQuade, Walter, ed. *Schoolhouse.* New York: Simon and Schuster, Inc., 1958.

Phenix, Philip H. *Education and the Common Good.* New York: Harper & Brothers, 1961.

Spears, Harold. *Curriculum Planning Through In-Service Programs.* Englewood Cliffs, N. J.: Prentice-Hall, Inc., 1957.

EPILOGUE:

CURRICULUM BUILDING REACHES TOWARD MATURITY

Writing this book has been an enriching, stimulating experience. My plan was to cut away as much as possible of the inordinate amount of detail that usually engulfs most books on the subject and to clarify and simplify the admittedly complex core of schooling—the curriculum. Hopefully, this book will serve as an introduction to a fascinating field of study, without losing interested students in the quicksand of excessive detail and overdocumentation. The framework necessary for an understanding of curriculum has been presented and discussed in the hope that readers may find a springboard for action. Then, after people get some feeling of security in curriculum work, details and documentation may serve to deepen the understanding of those who aspire to curriculum leadership roles. If this book produces some understanding and action in curriculum building, by interested persons from within and outside the school, it will have served its purpose well.

CURRICULUMS OF THE PAST

From our curriculum heritage we draw some practices that are sound and many that are highly questionable in the light of available modern knowledge. Out of the past comes excessive attention to minor details, rote memorization, rigid disciplinary practices, tightly compartmentalized branches of subject matter, and a highly overgeneralized system of marking or grading pupils. We find some schools that still operate with inflexible rules and regulations that make no allowance for human error. Arbitrary standards still divide children into grades with little or no consideration for open-ended learning experiences to enable forward movement for pupils capable of rapid progress. In the same graded situations, inadequate attention is often given to pupils who need extra help from the teacher. In some schools we still retain and practice a stimulus-response theory of human behavior that encouraged us to treat all children as though they would respond almost identically to any given stimulus. This theory is partly right but inadequate to the needs of today. The more recent perception-response theory of phenomenological psychology seems much more in keeping with the professed goals of modern education.

Curriculums of the past overemphasized intellectual and behavioral conformity in the schools; yet, we say we value uniqueness in individuals. Educational innoculation of all pupils by certain basic subject-matter areas was supposed to guarantee a common general education—whether or not that education was wanted or needed by pupils. Heavy emphasis upon mass group-testing programs represents another piece of baggage that still burdens some school systems. Rethinking some of these ideas and retooling some of these practices in the light of contemporary knowledge may offer more effective uses for those worth retaining. Those not worth retaining should be removed from practice and placed in the educational archives as reference data for educational historians.

Schools are not production lines to mass produce graduates in the way that the automobile manufacturers mass produce their annual models. Techniques of management and production that apply well to material goods are seldom applicable to the education of human beings. Tendencies of the past to copy and to import wholesale into the schools certain business and industrial management practices have prohibited sound growth and experimental practices in curriculum development. Quality of individual educational achievement, in a curriculum designed to meet individual needs, cannot be achieved until we recognize the school for what it is and deal with it accordingly. In schools we deal with infinitely precious human personality in a quest for growth, learning, and fulfillment. To help learners move toward their goals is an individualized process, not a mass endeavor. A major function of the schools is educating and nourishing individual uniqueness, not mass producing hordes of diploma- or degree-holding automatons.

CURRICULUMS OF THE PRESENT

Contemporary curriculums are in a transitional phase of development. Much that was considered valid in the past remains as the foundation of instructional programs. Recent emphasis upon secondary-school curriculum change has been a reform-type of movement in a few academic subjects. Although it is extremely difficult to see beyond today, all of us involved in education need to make some basic decisions about the direction that curriculums should take to try to meet the future effectively.

Older practices are being questioned and discarded in some schools. In a few schools, more modern approaches to content and method are being tried in pilot studies. These pilot programs represent one kind of educational research that is badly needed to give direction to improved school practices, for we no longer have time or energy to waste upon using something hailed as "modern and new" simply because it carries that label. We need evidence that newer programs will produce better results.

Too often our philosophy and practice have tended to swing erratically from one extreme to the other. This is a time for progress with balance in curriculum growth and design. Many research studies have been done with pupils and in schools that were atypical. Because of the poor choices of schools and pupils, few findings of value were ever incorporated in typical school situations. Contemporary researchers may have to change the type of school used and the nature of the questions asked, if they hope to have findings begin to change practices. School personnel tend to identify with other schools like their own, not with schools that are in favored locations, with more-than-average income families, and more-than-average budgets that provide a pupil population quite different from the typical public school.

CURRICULUMS OF THE FUTURE

Looking into the future in times like these is a risky venture; yet, look we must. Those who build curriculums find it wise and effective, as they seek sources from which to draw necessary data for curriculum improvement, to look backward at tradition and history, to look closely at the present, and then to look forward into the future. As the writer looks at present practices in reference to their potential to shape future curriculums, several promising trends appear that should help to make tomorrow's curriculums better and more effective than any preceding ones.

Efforts by researchers, teachers, and administrators to test new patterns for organizing school time, teaching talent, and pupil talent appear to be gaining ground. Desirable recommendations from these experimental studies may become common practice in many schools in the next decade. The length of school periods will probably be tailored to suit the nature of the learning experience. Periods of identical length in the secondary schools, for instance, will probably give way to an assorted number of different time periods with each being designed for a particular kind of learning activity. Obviously, such changes will demand a complicated class-scheduling process for pupils, and if present automation trends continue, the scheduling of pupils may be done by machines. The over-all effect of such changes may open channels and time for greater attention to individually tailored instructional programs for individual pupils.

Movement toward ungrading the public school should increase with additional data becoming available from evaluative studies of programs now in existence. As our schools move toward ungrading themselves, the time schedule and instructional programs will be designed to serve better the needs of specific kinds of learners. Instead of rigid grade divisions, we will find levels of learning groups and different phases of learning levels within the same classroom. Some academically talented pupils should complete the required twelve years of public schooling in considerably less time. Other pupils who are slow in grasping academic learning will probably take additional time to complete a core of basic knowledge and skills designed especially for their interests and abilities.

Continued progress toward improving the continuity of educational experiences should be apparent in the future. Studies examining the structure of subject matter have already shown us that our former placement of some content may have underestimated learning abilities of pupils. Relationships between different subject-matter areas need further study. Perhaps we may find many common elements that can be blended into a unified series of experiences from which pupils may derive an educational wholeness unlike any so far achieved.

Present trends toward pushing subject matter down from the university to the high school, and from the high school to the elementary school, need thorough, cautious, and detailed investigation. Although some elementary-school children may be able to learn certain advanced subject matter reduced to terms they can understand, evidence is lacking that such knowledge has any real value for young children. Childhood comes but once in a lifetime. Pushing information at children that makes them assume more mature mental outlooks before they are physically and emotionally mature enough to know what to do with them may harm children and rob them of the only period of their lives in which there should be room and time to grow without undue pressure.

Many educational, community-welfare, church, and governmental agencies see common problems in our schools. In spite of the fact that they see them from different perspectives today, tomorrow may bring a more common viewpoint. From such a base should come increased cooperative efforts to alleviate difficulties. Private foundations will continue to offer help to our schools and colleges; their interest and financial aid may act as a catalytic agent for improved school practices. Parents and other lay citizens are becoming much better informed about school problems and much more interested in them. If professional school personnel provide careful guidance and adequate information for these interested people, they should be increasingly helpful in giving practical advice to future curriculum builders.

Forces from within the school and outside the school are starting to work together to help the school improve its curriculum. The perfect curriculum will never be achieved, since it is an educational ideal toward which we must always move. However, if we keep our hearts, minds, and hands busy, we *can* improve our curriculums. Out of our efforts will come progress bringing us closer to the ideal, curriculums that will be worthy of the name—design for learning.

INDEX